AWESOME QUIZ Challenge!

AWESOME QUIZ Challenge!

Camilla de la Bedoyere

Discovery
CHANNEL™

Miles Kelly

First published in 2014 by Miles Kelly Publishing Ltd
Harding's Barn, Bardfield End Green, Thaxted, Essex, CM6 3PX, UK

2 4 6 8 10 9 7 5 3 1

Publishing Director Belinda Gallagher
Creative Director Jo Cowan
Managing Editor Amanda Askew
Editors Fram Bromage, Sarah Parkin
Cover Designer Simon Lee
Designer Rob Hale
Image Manager Liberty Newton
Production Manager Elizabeth Collins
Reprographics Stephan Davis

ISBN 978-1-78209-170-7

Printed in China

British Library Cataloguing-in-Publication Data
A catalogue record for this book is available from the British Library

Made with paper from a sustainable forest

www.mileskelly.net   info@mileskelly.net

ACKNOWLEDGMENTS
The publishers would like to thank the following sources for the use of their photographs:
KEY: C=Corbis, D=Dreamstime, FLPA= Frank Lane Picture Library, F=Fotolia, GI=Getty Images, iS=iStock, NGC=National Geographic
Creative, NPL=Nature Picture Library, S=Shutterstock, SPL=Science Photo Library, T=Topfoto
BACK COVER: Dmitry Yashkin/S, AndreAnita/S TITLE PAGE: Vladimir Wrangel/S, Eric Isselee/S, Mike Flippo/S, AHMAD FAIZAL
YAHYA/S, CLIPAREA Custom media/S, ILYA AKINSHIN/S CONTENTS: iStock EARTH'S WONDERS: Opener ozoptimist/S 1 iS 2 iS
3 pryzmat/S 4 Smileus/S 5 Tyler Boyes/S, Steffen Foerster/S, Tom Grundy/S, Tyler Boyes/S, Bragin Alexey/S, Manamana/S,
Christopher Kolaczan/S, Tyler Boyes/S, Marco Cavina/S, F, Vladimir Sazonov/S, Tyler Boyes/S, Tyler Boyes/S, USGS 7 Galyna
Andrushko/S 8 Nataliya Hora/S 9 Anton Foltin/S 10 EcoPrint/S 11 ozoptimist/S, Mark Schwettmann/S, JOEL SARTORE/NGC, S, S,
Vaclav Volrab/S, Nazzu/S, Tyler Olson/S, Rainer Albiez/S, ABC.pics/S 12 Lee Prince/S 13 Kichigin/S 14 Incredible Arctic/S 16 3355m/S,
Finbarr O'Reilly/Reuters/C, Andy Rouse/NPL, GI, Stan Osolinski/GI AMAZING NATURE: Opener Rich Carey/S 17 Rich Carey/S
18 Gentoo Multimedia Limited/S 19 S 20 Francois Loubser/S 21 nitrogenic.com/S 22 AndreAnita/S, F, Rich Carey/S, Txanbelin/S,
liveostockimages/S, Audrey Snider-Bell/S, covenant/S, Johan Swanepoel/S, Tom C Amon/S, Microstock Man/S, Steffen Foerster/S,
JonMilnes/S, iS, Eric Gevaert/S, Kane513/S 23 D 24 Eric Isselee/S 25 Richard Fitzer/S 27 BMJ/S, lightpoet/S, Thomas
Marent/Minden Pictures/NGC, Theodore Mattas/S, Linn Currie/S, Arto Hakola/S, kkaplin/S, Cathy Keifer/S, Arnoud Quanjer/S, Beverly
Joubert/NGC, Mircea Bezergheanu/S, Sari ONeal/S 28 Smileus/S 29 Lindsey Eltinge/S 30 Webitect/S 31 J. Helgason/S 32 Doug
Perrine/NPL, Iafoto/S, Ingo Arndt/Minden Pictures/FLPA, Hiroya Minakuchi/Minden Pictures/FLPA, gubh83/S, GEORGETTE
DOUWMA/NPL, NatalieJean/S BODY SCIENCE: Opener Tatiana Makotra/S 33 Germanskydiver/S 35 Tatiana Makotra/S
36 photosync/S 37 Phase4Studios/S 38 S, Milunkic/S, Alex Mit/S, Kannanimages/S, S, vasabii/S, dream designs/S, dream designs/S,
SARANS/S, Alex Mit/S, dream designs/S, CLIPAREA Custom media/S, Sebastian Kaulitzki/S 39 Thorsten Rust/S 40 Alex Mit/S
41 schankz/S 42 SebGross/S 43 leonello calvetti/S, zimowa/S, Anna Sedneva/S, iS, paintings/S, szefei/S, MichaelTaylor3d/S, Andrea
Danti/S, Lightspring/S, Sebastian Kaulitzki/S, Kondor83/S, CAROLINA BIOLOGICAL SUPPLY CO/VISUALS UNLIMITED, INC/SPL
44 Yellowj/S 45 DenisNata/S 46 S 47 sfam_photo/S 48 DON FAWCETT/SPL, FRIEDRICH SAURER/SPL, Franck Boston/S, Olga
Lipatova/S, THOMAS DEERINCK, NCMIR/SPL, PROFESSORS P.M. MOTTA, P.M. ANDREWS, K.R. PORTER & J. VIAL/SPL
SPEED MACHINES: Opener Darren Brode/S 49 NASA 50 Sergei Bachlakov/S 51 Chris Parypa Photography/S 52 Hodag Media/S
53 Jorg Hackemann/S 54 Lee Prince/S, Graham Bloomfield/S, Rosli Othman/S, NASA, Dmitry Yashkin/S, Laurence Gough/S,
Natursports/S, CHEN WS/S, NASA, NASA, Helena Darvelid/Vestas Sailrocket, Jorge Salcedo/S, NASA-DFRC, Marcio Jose Bastos
Silva/S, Max Earey/S, DenisKlimov/S 55 bluehand/S 56 Tamara Kulikova/S 57 AHMAD FAIZAL YAHYA/S 58 NASA 59 Chris Parypa
Photography/S, NASA, NASA, Darren Brode/S, Brian Finestone/S, MAC1/S, Charles Chen Art/S, Sam Moores/S, Michael Stokes/S,
Darryl Brooks/S 60 AHMAD FAIZAL YAHYA/S 61 Kitch Bain/S 62 Ibooo7/S, 64 Graham Bloomfield/S, Josh Cassatt/Navy.mil, GI,
rodho/S THRILL SEEKERS: Opener ChristopheMichot/S, 65 sss615/S 66 Thomas Zobl/S 67 Franck Boston/S 68 Maxisport/S
70 Mike Gorman/S, Jan Cejka/S, dboystudio/S, Vilant/S, JonMilnes/S, Christophe Michot/S, Mavrick/S, s_bukley/S, Wolf/C, Dainis
Derics/S, Dennis Donohue/S, Vitalii Nesterchuk/S, D, steveball/S, Rommel Canlas/S, David Crockett/S 72 NASA 73 Neale Cousland/S
75 Germanskydiver/S, Hulton-Deutsch Collection/C, Zack Frank/S, Sean Nel/S, Mike Liu/S, dibrova/S, NASA, Tyler Olson/S, T, tatiana
sayig/S, Fotolia, evantravels/S 77 Erika Cross/S 79 cdrin/S, 80 Hugh Sitton/C, A Cotton Photo/S, REX/c.National Geographic/Everett
UNEARTH HISTORY: Opener Narongsak Nagadhana/S 81 MindStorm/S 82 leoks/S 83 lexan/S 84 Natalia Bratslavsky/S
86 saiko3p/S, Hung Chung Chih/S, Alan Lucas/S, Georgescu Gabriel/S, Giancarlo Liguori/S, Mirek Hejnicki/S, Tatiana Popova/S,
Muzhik/S, Irina Burakova/S, Zack Frank/S, Roger-Viollet/T, Tom Till/SuperStock/C, Jeff Whyte/S, Ziye/S, The Granger Collection/T
87 TrotzOlga/S 88 D 90 Lukiyanova Natalia/frenta/S 91 Justin Black/S, Pecold/S, The Granger Collection/T, Vladimir
Korostyshevskiy/S, World History Archive/T, Arthur R/S, Narongsak Nagadhana/S, vig64/S, Gwoeii/S, Luciano Mortula/S, Vladimir
Korostyshevskiy/S, SeanPavonePhoto/S 93 ChameleonsEye/S 95 Anna Jurkovska/S 96 gary yim/S, Amanda Nicholls/S, Yuri
Yavnik/S, Igor Plotnikov/S, ChaosMaker/S

All other photographs are from digitalSTOCK, digitalvision, John Foxx, PhotoAlto, PhotoDisc, PhotoEssentials, PhotoPro, Stockbyte

Every effort has been made to acknowledge the source and copyright holder of each picture.

Miles Kelly Publishing apologises for any unintentional errors or omissions.

Contents

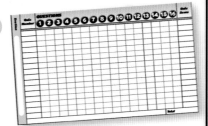

How to **Play**

Choose which section you'd like to play. There are six sections, each with 16 quizzes.

The Question & Answer Quizzes are A, B, or C, True or False?, Lucky Dip, Odd One Out, Name the Number, Starting with, Be a Genius, What am I?, Where am I?, and Who am I?

The Picture Challenge Quizzes are What am I? and Picture It.

The final type of quiz is Total Recall.

Use the scorecard at the back of the book to mark your results and see if you're a quiz master or if you need to swot up on some awesome facts!

Question & Answer **QUIZZES**

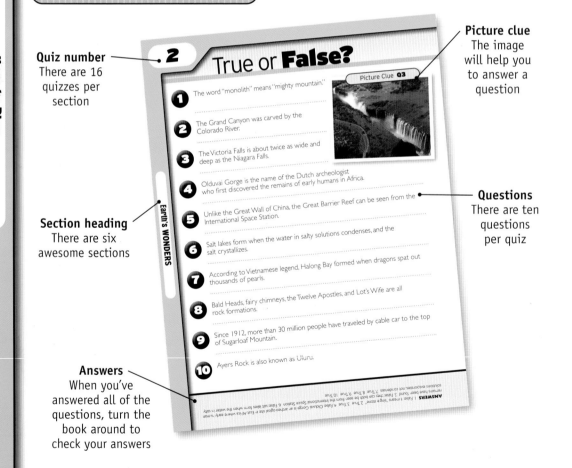

Quiz number
There are 16 quizzes per section

Section heading
There are six awesome sections

Answers
When you've answered all of the questions, turn the book around to check your answers

Picture clue
The image will help you to answer a question

Questions
There are ten questions per quiz

2 True or **False?**

Picture Clue Q3

1. The word "monolith" means "mighty mountain."

2. The Grand Canyon was carved by the Colorado River.

3. The Victoria Falls is about twice as wide and deep as the Niagara Falls.

4. Olduvai Gorge is the name of the Dutch archeologist who first discovered the remains of early humans in Africa.

5. Unlike the Great Wall of China, the Great Barrier Reef can be seen from the International Space Station.

6. Salt lakes form when the water in salty solutions condenses, and the salt crystallizes.

7. According to Vietnamese legend, Halong Bay formed when dragons spat out thousands of pearls.

8. Bald Heads, fairy chimneys, the Twelve Apostles, and Lot's Wife are all rock formations.

9. Since 1912, more than 30 million people have traveled by cable car to the top of Sugarloaf Mountain.

10. Ayers Rock is also known as Uluru.

Earth's WONDERS

ANSWERS: 1. False 1 means "single stone". 2. True 3. True 4. False Olduvai Gorge is an archeological site in East Africa where early human remains have been found. 5. False they can both be seen from the International Space Station. 6. False salt lakes form when the water is salty solutions evaporates, not condenses 7. True 8. True 9. True 10. True

How to Play

Picture Challenge **QUIZZES**

Picture clue
The images will help you to work out the answers

Questions
There are 12–16 questions per quiz

Total Recall **QUIZZES**

Questions
There are ten questions to test your recall skills on what you've just read

Fact page
Read this page first and try to remember the facts before you quiz yourself

Earth's WONDERS

Bruce Canyon in Utah, U.S., is full of needlelike pinnacles called hoodoos. These structures form when the rock is eroded by rain and frost.

A, B, or C

1 The desert area of Wadi Rum in Jordan was the location for which film?
a *Tron* **b** *Prometheus* **c** *Transformers: Revenge of the Fallen*

2 The Matterhorn mountain is on the border between which two countries?
a Switzerland and Italy **b** Switzerland and Austria **c** Italy and France

3 Which of these islands is the largest?
a Greenland **b** Madagascar **c** Borneo

4 Which of these mammals can be found in Madagascar?
a Lemurs **b** Llamas **c** Lynxes

5 Where might you witness the midnight sun?
a Svalbard **b** Isambard **c** The Bard of Avon

6 The world's largest active volcano is in Hawaii. What is it called?
a Mauna Kea **b** Mona Lisa **c** Mauna Loa

7 In what type of rocky landscape might you see cenotes, caves, and stalactites?
a Granite **b** Limestone **c** Arkose

8 What is the traditional Aboriginal name for Ayers Rock?
a Aloha **b** Aloe Vera **c** Uluru

9 What is molten rock called?
a Magnetite **b** Magma **c** Magnesium

10 Where would you be if you were sunbathing on Copacabana Beach?
a Rio de Janeiro **b** Cuba **c** Copenhagen

Picture Clue **Q10**

Earth's WONDERS

True or **False?**

1 The word "monolith" means "mighty mountain."
....

2 The Grand Canyon was carved by the Colorado River.
....

Picture Clue **Q3**

3 The Victoria Falls is about twice as wide and deep as the Niagara Falls.
....

4 Olduvai Gorge is the name of the Dutch archeologist who first discovered the remains of early humans in Africa.
....

5 Unlike the Great Wall of China, the Great Barrier Reef can be seen from the International Space Station.
....

6 Salt lakes form when the water in salty solutions condenses, and the salt crystallizes.
....

7 According to Vietnamese legend, Halong Bay formed when dragons spat out thousands of pearls.
....

8 Bald Heads, fairy chimneys, the Twelve Apostles, and Lot's Wife are all rock formations.
....

9 Since 1912, more than 30 million people have traveled by cable car to the top of Sugarloaf Mountain.
....

10 Ayers Rock is also known as Uluru.

ANSWERS 1. False: it means "single stone". 2.True 3.True 4. False: Olduvai Gorge is an archeological site in East Africa where early human remains have been found. 5. False: they can both be seen from the International Space Station. 6. False: salt lakes form when the water in salty solutions evaporates, not condenses 7.True 8.True 9.True 10.True

Lucky **Dip**

1 Name the seven colors in a rainbow.

....

2 ROVs are used to search places where humans cannot go, such as the deep ocean. What does ROV stand for?

....

3 What name is given to a fog or haze that is mixed with smoke, or other pollutants?

....

4 Neap, spring, and breaker are all types of tide. True or false?

....

5 The world's deepest mine is Tau Tona in South Africa. What is mined there— coal or gold?

....

6 By what name is the ocean's mesopelagic zone also known—the vampire zone, the twilight zone, or the leviathan zone?

....

Picture Clue **Q7**

7 What F is a living thing that has been preserved within a rock?

....

8 Which line of latitude is north of the equator, Tropic of Cancer or Tropic of Capricorn?

....

9 Diamond is the hardest mineral, but what is the softest?

....

10 What is Earth's solid, rocky crust called—the troposphere, lithosphere, or mesosphere?

Earth's WONDERS

ANSWERS 1. Red, orange, yellow, green, blue, indigo, violet. 2. Remotely Operated Vehicle 3. Smog 4. False: breakers are types of wave 5. Gold 6. Twilight zone 7. Fossil 8. Tropic of Cancer 9. Talc 10. Lithosphere

Odd One **Out**

1 Grossglockner, Eiger, Kosciuszko—which of these mountains is not in the Alps?

....

2 Which of these natural events does not happen at sea—tsunami, hurricane, or solifluction?

....

3 Tagus, Euphrates, Okavango—which of these rivers is in Africa?

....

4 Only one of these rocks can be described as igneous—limestone, gabbro, or schist. Which one?

....

5 Which of these global wind system names is genuine—Roaring Forties, Naughty Nineties, or Swinging Sixties?

....

6 Which of these Great Lakes has an area of less than 12,000 sq mi (20,000 sq km)—Erie, Ontario, or Huron?

....

7 Mount Pinatubo, Mauna Loa, Mount Kenya—only one of these volcanoes is inactive. Which one?

....

8 Which of these is not a type of grassland—steppe, savanna, or verdigris?

....

9 Cirrus, stratus, cumulus—only one of these is a high level cloud. Which one?

....

10 Which explorer did not give his name to a sea—Magellan, Barents, or Weddell?

Picture Clue **Q9**

Name the **Number**

1 The Tunguska Event in Siberia flattened trees in a huge area. It was probably caused by an asteroid. What was the year?

....

2 The Haiti earthquake had devastating effects, leaving more than 1.6 million homeless. In which year did this disaster occur?

....

3 In which year did the Yellow River Floods in China kill between one and two million people?

....

4 On December 26 of which year did the Indian Ocean Tsunami cause widespread death and destruction?

....

5 The San Francisco earthquake caused fires that destroyed much of the city. What was the year?

....

6 The deadliest cyclone ever recorded killed up to 500,000 people. Which year did it hit East Pakistan—1970 or 1980?

....

7 The eruption of Krakatoa made the largest noise ever heard and set off enormous tsunamis. What was the year?

....

8 Hurricane Katrina was one of the strongest hurricanes to ever hit the U.S. In what year did it destroy much of New Orleans?

....

9 The east coast of the U.S. was paralyzed by The Great Blizzard in which year?

....

10 In what year did Australia's Black Saturday bushfires occur, killing 173 people?

Earth's WONDERS

What am I?

1 I am the most common of all volcanic rocks. I form when lava seeps up where tectonic plates pull apart.

2 I am the most common mineral in Earth's crust.

3 I am a soft metal and I can be found in small grains in rivers. I am mainly used to make jewelry.

4 I am formed when layer upon layer of mud settles on seabeds and lake beds.

5 I am a sedimentary rock made up of grains of sand laid down in deserts, under the sea, or by ice sheets.

6 I am an igneous rock formed from magma that solidifies before it reaches the surface.

7 I am a precious red gem, usually found in riverbeds.

8 I am the world's hardest mineral. I form over billions of years under huge pressure. I am a highly prized gemstone.

9 When limestone comes into contact with hot magma, it is "cooked" and forms me. I am often used in sculpture.

13 When a grain gets inside an oyster shell, the oyster smothers it in liquid to stop it irritating. This liquid hardens to make me.

10 I am a form of quartz that has been stained purple by traces of iron.

14 I am a sedimentary rock. I form from skeletons of tiny organisms that lived 100 million years ago. I am often used to write on a blackboard.

11 I am mainly found as an ore (combined with another element). I am often used to make pipes.

15 I am the softest of all minerals. I can hold fragrance, so I am used to make cosmetics.

12 I am formed when sticky, liquid tree resin hardens and fossilizes over thousands of years.

16 My grains are so fine that when wet, I feel like smooth, slippery plasticine.

ANSWERS 1. Basalt 2. Quartz 3. Gold 4. Shale 5. Sandstone 6. Granite 7. Ruby 8. Diamond 9. Marble 10. Amethyst 11. Copper 12. Amber 13. Pearl 14. Chalk 15. Talc 16. Clay

Starting with **R**

Earth's WONDERS

1 What R is the rock face that has the faces of four American presidents carved into it?

....

Picture Clue **Q1**

2 Name the arch of colors that can appear in the sky on a rainy day.

....

3 What was the surname of Charles, an American geologist whose scale is a measure of earthquake energy?

....

4 What type of valley is caused by the downward displacement of a massive block of Earth's surface?

....

5 What name is given to an ocean phenomenon where storm waves stack together to form giant walls of water?

....

6 Which natural habitat thrives in tropical places that enjoy plenty of daily rainfall?

....

7 Which country is one of the world's top diamond producers?

....

8 Which chemical element was once used as a source of radiation for radiotherapy?

....

9 Which European river flows from the Swiss Alps to the North Sea coast of the Netherlands?

....

10 Petroglyphs and pictographs are examples of what type of art, favored by Aborigines of Australia?

ANSWERS 1. Rushmore (Mount) 2. Rainbow 3. Richter 4. Rift 5. Rogue wave 6. Rain forest 7. Russia 8. Radium 9. Rhine 10. Rock art

Be a **Genius**

1 What word describes the way rocks can be stretched and deformed under extremes of temperature and pressure—ductile or textile?

....

2 Mountains are made of rocks that are folded up, or down. What is an anticline—an upfold or a downfold?

....

3 What is the world's tallest mountain?

....

Picture Clue **Q4**

4 On what continent would you find the Alps?

....

5 What is the world's longest mountain range?

....

6 Which mountain range separates Europe from Asia?

....

7 K2 is the world's second highest mountain. How tall is it, to the nearest 300 ft (100 m)?

....

8 What is the name of the highest peak in the Rocky Mountains?

....

9 What C is the name given to any group of parallel mountain ranges?

....

10 Which Austrian geologist pioneered the study of the Alps and named the supercontinent Gondwanaland?

Where am I?

Earth's WONDERS

1 I am exploring one of the the world's most isolated islands. There are strange-looking stone statues to keep me company.

2 I am on a mountain in a U.S. state, where there are more rainy days than anywhere else in the world, with an average of 335 per year.

3 I am swimming in the world's largest ocean. It contains about 163 million cu mi (679.6 million cu km) of water.

4 It is hot and dry here, in Asia's largest desert.

5 The water in this shrinking lake is 8.6 times saltier than that of most oceans, and I can float easily.

6 On average, it rains here just one day in every six years. Which South American country am I in?

7 Standing on the top of the highest mountain in the Alps gives me astonishing views. What peak am I standing on?

8 It is cold for most of the year here, and there are few animals and plants. I am on the world's largest island.

9 I am in Africa, on the banks of the world's longest river.

Picture Clue **Q10**

10 I am in the world's sunniest place, where there is an average of 4,127 hours of sunshine a year.

ANSWERS 1. Easter Island 2. Mount Waialeale, Hawaii 3. The Pacific Ocean 4. Gobi Desert 5. The Dead Sea 6. Chile (in a place called Arica) 7. Mont Blanc 8. Greenland 9. River Nile 10. Arizona (in a place called Yuma)

True or **False?**

1 Coral reefs are built by tiny animals called polymers.

....

2 In 1984, a hailstorm in Munich brought down the air traffic control tower.

....

3 A swamp that develops where salty sea water meets fresh river water is called a mangabey.

....

Picture Clue **Q3**

4 About 250 million years ago, there was just one single landmass, called Pangaea.

....

5 Twelve rocky stacks, known as the Dirty Dozen, stand along the coastline on Port Campbell National Park in Australia.

....

6 Oceans make up around 70 percent of Earth's surface.

....

7 Tornadoes are measured using the Fujita Scale.

....

8 Sand dunes are made of tiny grains of diamond.

....

9 In 1888, a storm in India produced hailstones the size of oranges.

....

10 The coldest known place in the world is Vostok Station in Antarctica.

Earth's WONDERS

Picture **It**

1 In what country would you find this massive monolith?

2 What are these strange rock pinnacles called?

3 In which city would you see this statue?

4 What is Africa's highest peak?

5 In what continent do Pantanal cowboys work?

6 What two countries border the Niagara Falls?

7 In what country would you find Wadi Rum?

 8 What name do Italians give the Matterhorn?

 9 On what island might a lemur sit beneath a baobab tree?

 10 What is Svalbard's largest island called?

11 What name is given to molten volcanic rock?

12 What is the largest coral reef system in the world?

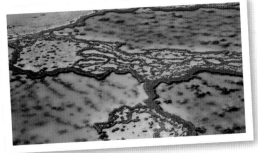

Be a **Genius**

1 Some people claim that budgerigars, toads, and snakes have predicted earthquakes. True or false?

2 In the event of a hurricane, should you go to a building's roof or center?

3 When did the last period of mass extinctions happen on Earth?

4 What travels fastest—a meteorite crashing to Earth or an open-ocean tsunami?

Picture Clue **Q6**

5 An active volcano is one that has erupted in living memory. True or false?

6 Which national park in Wyoming, U.S., contains a supervolcano and hundreds of geysers?

7 Which Sumatran volcano erupted about 74,000 years ago and nearly wiped out all of humanity?

8 Which civilization had a calendar that was wrongly said to forecast the end of the world in 2012?

9 If the Large Hadron Collider accidentally created a mini black hole, what would happen to it?

10 Which catastrophic event is expected to happen first?
a Our galaxy collides with the Andromeda Galaxy **b** The Sun will expand and engulf Earth

ANSWERS 1. True 2. Center 3. It's happening now 4. Tsunami 5. False it is one that has erupted at least once in the last 10,000 years 6. Yellowstone 7. Mount Toba 8. The Mayans 9. It would evaporate 10. a The collision is predicted in 4 billion years and solar expansion 1–3 billion years later

1 What weather event is accompanied by force 12 winds, causes widespread devastation, and destroys buildings?

....

2 The Harmony is a hot, dry wind that crosses the Sahara. True or false?

....

3 How many sides do most snowflakes have—4, 5, or 6?

....

4 What type of power uses the Sun's energy to make electricity?

Picture Clue **Q3**

....

5 What D describes the process by which large areas of forest are destroyed?

....

6 Which word does not describe a type of forest—cloud, rain, or wind?

....

7 What name is given to a giant river of ice?

....

8 Over time, tiny dead ocean animals and plants can turn into oil and gas. True or false?

....

9 What instrument do scientists use to measure vibrations in the ground— seismographs or barometers?

....

10 Which natural phenomenon kills more people and causes more damage to property than any other?
a Volcanic eruptions **b** Tornadoes **c** Floods

Earth's WONDERS

Where am I?

Earth's WONDERS

1 I am a large island called Spitsbergen, surrounded by glaciers. Which island group am I part of?

2 I am watching curtains of color shimmer across the sky. Am I at the North Pole or the Equator?

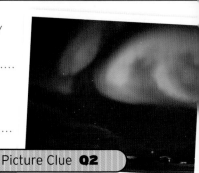

3 I am standing in the world's largest desert, surrounded by sand dunes. Where am I?

Picture Clue **02**

4 I am watching lava flowing out of the world's largest active volcano. Am I in Hawaii or Washington, U.S.?

5 I am watching water cascade over the edge of the Victoria Falls, but I am not in Zimbabwe. What country am I in?

6 I am looking at the Tsingy Peaks, on a vast island in the Indian Ocean. What is the island called?

7 I am in mountain range that began to form about 90 million years ago in Europe and contains the continent's largest mountains. What is it called?

8 I am in a country where tourists can visit fairy chimneys in Goreme National Park. Where am I?

9 I am blinded by the startling white landscape of Salar de Uyuni in Bolivia. What type of geographical feature am I looking at—an ice sheet or a salt lake?

10 I am in the world's largest-known freshwater wetland. What is it called?

ANSWERS 1. Svalbard 2. North Pole 3. Sahara desert 4. Hawaii (at Mauna Loa) 5. Zambia 6. Madagascar 7. The Alps 8. Turkey 9. Salt lake 10. Pantanal

Name the **Number**

1 How many lightning strikes hit the Grand Canyon each year, to the nearest 1000—26,000 or 260,000?

....

2 How long has it been since Earth's magnetic poles flipped—700,000 years or 200,000 years?

....

3 Which number on the earthquake Richter Scale is defined as "Serious damage over hundreds of miles?"

....

4 The Great Barrier Reef contains thousands of reefs and islands. Does it stretch for 240 mi (390 km) or 1,240 mi (2,000 km)?

....

5 How long ago did Earth form—4.5 billion years ago or 4.5 million years ago?

....

6 How many slices of bread could be toasted using the energy in a single lightning bolt?

....

7 How many times more powerful was the eruption of Mount St. Helen's in 1980 than the atom bomb dropped on Hiroshima—100 times or 500 times?

....

8 To the nearest 10, how many thunderstorms strike Earth every hour?

....

9 A major volcanic eruption might produce one km^3 of material. How much might a supervolcano produce—1,000 km^3 or 10,000 km^3?

....

10 How many seconds' warning did Japanese people have of the massive 2011 Tokyo earthquake?

Earth's WONDERS

WONDER
No More

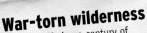

▼ Parts of Virunga National Park have been devastated by the clearing of land for farming using "slash-and-burn."

We are changing our planet at a rate that has only been equalled in the past by cataclysmic events, such as massive meteorite impacts and supervolcano eruptions. Only future generations will fully comprehend the damage we are doing to some of Earth's most awesome places.

War-torn wilderness

Despite suffering a century of poaching and years of war, the small population of mountain gorillas in Virunga National Park, in the Democratic Republic of the Congo, clings to life. However, the habitat is under relentless pressure from the growing human population, and large areas of forest have been destroyed.

▼ Belize corals are being bleached (killed) by a combination of pollution and rising temperatures.

▶ The Virunga National Park is the oldest reserve in Africa and is home to around 100 mountain gorillas.

Everglades forever?

For the last 70 years, developers have been draining Florida's Everglades swamps to build on the reclaimed land, and water has been diverted from the swamps to supply agriculture and urban areas. The effects have been described as environmental ruin.

Watery grave

The corals of Belize have been described as the most outstanding barrier reef in the Northern Hemisphere and a significant habitat for endangered species, such as marine turtles, manatees, and American marine crocodiles.

▶ Slash pines growing in the freshwater areas of Florida create a habitat for birds and small mammals. The timber is also of commercial use.

1 In which American state might you visit the Everglades?

....

2 Is the sea around Belize famous for coral or glaciers?

....

3 What type of ecosystem is the Everglades—swamp or rain forest?

....

4 On which continent do gorillas live?

....

5 What word describes swamp land that has been drained?

....

6 Is Belize in the Southern or Northern Hemisphere?

....

7 What habitat is destroyed by "slash and burn?"

....

8 What B is the name given to the killing of corals?

....

9 In which country would you find the Virunga National Park?

....

10 What P is an environmental hazard that is adding to the loss of coral reefs?

Earth's WONDERS

Amazing
NATURE

The hawksbill turtle lives in tropical waters and is named after
the way its head ends in a point, like a bird's beak.

A, B, or C

1 Cuttlefish are closely related to…
a Jellyfish **b** Squid **c** Lobsters

2 Sockeye is a type of…
a Owl **b** Bear **c** Salmon

3 What does a lepidopterist study?
a Leopards **b** Bats **c** Butterflies

Picture Clue **Q1**

4 How far can an Arctic tern fly in just one year?
a 43,000 mi (70,000 km) **b** 14,000 mi (23,000 km) **c** 31,000 mi (50,000 km)

5 What is an inflorescence?
a Flower used to make perfume **b** Flowering structure **c** Underground fungus

6 What is a group of wolves called?
a Deck **b** Pack **c** Set

7 Where might you see mountain gorillas?
a Rajasthan **b** Yucatan **c** Rwanda

8 What is the fastest land animal over a long distance?
a Pronghorn **b** Cheetah **c** Arctic hare

9 Where would you find the most African elephants?
a Algeria **b** Botswana **c** The Ivory Coast

10 How long can male emperor penguins survive without food while incubating an egg?
a 34 days **b** 64 days **c** 94 days

Amazing NATURE

True or **False?**

1 Penguins live in the Arctic.

2 Salmon can change color from silvery blue to bright red and develop greenish heads.

3 Monarch butterflies detect geothermal radiation and use it to navigate when they migrate.

4 When a turtle outgrows its shell, it has to swim to shore to grow a new one.

5 Some wildebeest have evolved stripes so they can escape predators by hiding in a herd of zebras.

6 Tiger, bull, cat, dog, and bignose are all types of shark.

7 Periodical cicadas are bugs that only live during a full moon.

8 Spanish ibexes can grow horns that measure up to 30 in (75 cm).

Picture Clue **Q5**

9 Flamingos have pink plumage because they survive entirely on a diet of pink shrimps.

10 A single swarm of locusts may number 16 billion individuals.

Amazing NATURE

ANSWERS 1. False: they live in the Antarctic. 2. True 3. False: they use the Sun as a compass and Earth's magnetic field to navigate 4. False: a turtle's shell is part of its body and grows as it grows 5. False: sometimes zebra hide among wildebeest herds 6. True 7. False: they live underground as larvae for up to 17 years, then emerge as adults 8. True 9. False: they eat spirulina, cyanobacteria that contain pigment 10. True

Lucky **Dip**

1 Coral reefs are made by tiny living organisms that are related to sea anemones. What are they called?

....

2 What type of animal is a crab—a cnidarian, a hexapod, or a crustacean?

....

3 What D is the name given to the upright, triangular fin on a shark's back?

....

4 I have a wingspan of 11 ft (3.5 m), I feed on squid, and I inspired a poem by Samuel Taylor Coleridge. What bird am I?

....

5 Which of these animals is not a member of the bovid (cattle) family—bongo, tutu, kudu, dik-dik, or puku?

....

6 Pandas occasionally eat small animals. True or false?

....

7 Which of these animals lives in groups that are led by females, not males—elephant, gorilla, or wolf?

....

8 I am a large brown animal living in North America and I feast on salmon. What am I?

....

9 Penguins survive the cold because they have a thick layer of fur. True or false?

....

Picture Clue **Q9**

10 Which bird does not migrate long distances—woodpecker, snow goose, bar-tailed godwit, or Arctic tern?

Odd One **Out**

1 Which snake is the odd one out, and why—burmese python, adder, coral snake?

....

2 Which of these animals doesn't live in Australia—parma wallaby, long-nosed echidna, or common wombat?

....

3 Which one of these animals does not form huge flying swarms— locust, red-billed quelea, or jewel wasp?

....

4 Corpse flower, venus flytrap, and pitcher plant—which plant is not carnivorous?

....

5 Which of these animals doesn't hunt in groups—hyena, polar bear, or orca?

....

6 Which of these birds is the odd one out, and why—ostrich, buzzard, or penguin?

....

Picture Clue Q6

7 Horsetail, bamboo, wheat—one of these plants does not belong to the grass family. Which one?

....

8 Which of these species has not been declared extinct—west African black rhino, barbary lion, or Javan rhino?

....

9 Which of these marine mammals feeds by filtering small prey from the water— humpback whale, beluga, or sperm whale?

....

10 Which substance is not essential for plants to photosynthesize? Carbon dioxide, soil, or sunlight?

Name the **Number**

1 Vertebrates are divided into groups. How many groups are there?

....

2 How many dorsal fins does a great white shark have?

....

3 How long was the dinosaur *Brachiosaurus*— more or less than 65 ft (20 m)?

....

Picture Clue **Q2**

4 How tall is the world's tallest tree. Is it 368 ft (112 m) or 638 ft (195 m)?

....

5 How many offspring could one bacterium produce, in theory, if it reproduces every 20 minutes for 24 hours—5 trillion, 5 billion trillion, or 10 trillion trillion?

....

6 How many species of fungi have been identified so far—10,000 or 100,000?

....

7 The largest mollusk is a colossal squid. How many tentacles does it have?

....

8 *Mamenchisaurus* had the longest neck of any known dinosaur. How many vertebrae bones did it have in its neck—12 or 19?

....

9 How old is the world's oldest living tree—almost 5,000 or 50,000 years old?

....

10 Starfish show pentameric symmetry. How many "arms" do they have?

Amazing NATURE

1 I am a flightless bird. Some might say that I am regal.

2 I will soon grow wings as I turn into another animal.

3 I am a reptile that lives in the ocean.

4 I am a large African antelope.

5 I am a fish that swims in a huge group. My name begins with S.

6 I am a long reptile with a noisy tail.

7 I am a mammal with a very long neck.

8 I roll balls of dung to lay my eggs in.

9 I am an amphibian that lives in trees.

10 I carry my baby in a pouch on the front of my body.

11 I am a monkey with a colorful face and large teeth.

12 I am a fish. When I get angry or defensive, I swell up like a spiky balloon.

13 I am the largest carnivore in the world and live in the Arctic.

14 I am a striped predator with sharp claws and teeth.

15 My name means "river horse."

16 I am a reptile that can change color to match my surroundings.

ANSWERS 1. Royal penguin 2. Monarch caterpillar 3. Turtle 4. Wildebeest 5. Sardines 6. Rattlesnake 7. Giraffe 8. Dung beetle 9. Tree frog 10. Kangaroo 11. Mandrill 12. Pufferfish 13. Polar bear 14. Tiger 15. Hippopotamus 16. Chameleon

Starting with **B**

Amazing NATURE

1 An American buffalo is also known as what?

....

2 What do vertebrates have that invertebrates lack?

....

3 Which group of animals includes types that are called spectacled, sloth, sun, and Asiatic?

....

Picture Clue **Q3**

4 Bitterns, boobies, bateleurs, bustards, and budgerigars are all types of what?

....

5 What word describes an aquatic animal that is enclosed within two hinged shells?

....

6 The Brahminy snake, Mexican tetra fish, and star-nosed mole all have what in common?

....

7 What color is the chow-chow dog's tongue?

....

8 A family of young animals is referred to as what?

....

9 Which frogs are famous for their loud, booming croaks and their habit of preying upon small vertebrates?

....

10 Which insect group makes up the largest order of animals and is studied by coleopterists.

Be a **Genius**

1 Which are bigger—Asian or African elephants?

....

2 Elephant tusks are huge teeth. True or false?

....

3 What is the leader of an elephant herd called, a matriarch or a patriarch?

Picture Clue **Q2**

....

4 What is the natural lifespan of an African elephant (to the nearest five years)?

....

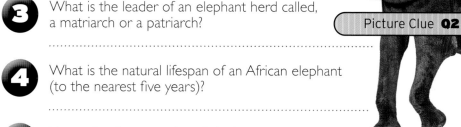

5 Name the three species of elephant.

....

6 What M is the time when male elephants are ready to mate?

....

7 All male and female elephants have tusks. True or false?

....

8 Do desert elephants have longer or shorter legs than other elephants?

....

9 What famous elephant gave its name to the English language, meaning anything that is extra big?

....

10 How tall was the largest elephant ever measured (from shoulder to forefoot), to the nearest 4 in (10 cm)?

Amazing NATURE

ANSWERS 1. African 2. True 3. Matriarch 4. 60 years 5. African bush elephant, African forest elephant, and Asian elephant 6. Musth 7. False: female Asian elephants usually lack tusks 8. Longer 9. Jumbo (the Circus Elephant) 10. 13 ft (396 cm)

What am I?

1 I am the largest animal on Earth. Even my baby is 23 ft (7 m) long.

2 My Latin name is *Panthera onca.* I'm a spotted member of the big cat family.

Picture Clue **Q1**

3 Some people call me an "upside down tree." I store water in my trunk and I'm a native of Madagascar.

4 I am an alga that grows in long filaments. My chloroplasts are arranged in a spiral.

5 I am one of the world's largest beetles and am named after a mythological hero of superhuman strength.

6 I am a social insect known for my stripes and sting. I collect pollen and carry it in pollen baskets on my legs.

7 I am an enormous reptile that can reach a great age. I live on islands that were visited by Charles Darwin.

8 I was introduced into Australia in 1935 to control cane beetles. Now I am a serious pest myself.

9 I lay tiny eggs, suck nectar from flowers, and can beat my wings up to 80 times a minute.

10 My name comes from the Greek for "prickly plant." My prickles are actually leaves.

ANSWERS 1. Blue whale 2. Jaguar 3. Baobab 4. Spyrogyra 5. Hercules beetle 6. Honey bee 7. Galapagos tortoise 8. Cane toad 9. Hummingbird 10. Cactus

True or **False?**

1 Some crabs use their giant claws to scare one another.

....

2 If all the world's bees died out, there is a good chance humans would starve to death.

....

3 Tiny shrews can twitch their whiskers 20 times a second.

....

4 Scientists think that humans carry the genes to regrow limbs.

....

5 Mistletoe is a parastic plant.

....

6 The world's biggest flower is as big as a bus.

....

7 Porcupine spines are made of bone.

....

8 Tarantula spiders can live longer than most pet dogs.

....

9 Some frogs can survive cold weather by turning to ice.

....

10 *Giganotosaurus* was a massive dinosaur and the biggest animal to ever live.

Picture Clue **Q10**

Amazing NATURE

Picture **It**

1 Are these emperor or macaroni penguins?

2 What does this long-nosed mammal eat?

3 The Hercules beetle is one of the strongest animals—for its size— on Earth. True or false?

4 Name these brightly colored birds.

5 What is the world's most abundant bird?

6 This long-distance bird is sometimes called a sea swallow. What is its real name?

7 What is this stinky plant called—Rafflesia or Effluvia?

10 This snake is squeezing its prey to death. Is it a python or a cobra?

8 Some plants eat meat. True or false?

11 Starfish can regrow their legs. True or false?

9 Name this speedy spotted cat.

12 This butterfly is famous for its lengthy migrations. What is it called?

Starting with **M**

1 What M is a group of pouched animals that live in Australia and surrounding islands?

2 What word describes the long journeys that some animals undertake in search of food, water, or mates?

3 What name is given to the hairy ancestors of our modern elephants?

4 Octopuses, slugs, and snails are all types of what— mollusk, macaque, or mantid?

Picture Clue **Q1**

5 Which monk studied pea plants to show that characteristics pass from one generation to the next, and is known as the father of genetics?

6 What type of fish is able to breathe air, climb out of water, and cling to branches with a sucker on its belly?

7 What deadly disease is transmitted by female mosquitoes?

8 Which large island is home to lemurs, baobabs, and tenrecs?

9 What M is a type of mammal, such as the duck-billed platypus, which lays eggs?

10 Which adult flying insect only lives for just one day, or even less?

Odd One **Out**

1 Which of these is not a bird—eagle, eagle owl, or eagle ray?

....

2 Which of these animals lives near the South Pole—polar bear, emperor penguin, or walrus?

....

3 Which of these is a fish—glasseye, glassfin, or glasstail?

....

4 Which of these cats is not native to Africa—tiger, leopard, or cheetah?

....

5 Which of these is not a type of pig—peccary, babirusa, or oryx?

....

6 Mynah, gray parrot, and tawny frogmouth—which one of these birds cannot mimic the human voice?

....

7 Which of these is not a type of crab—ghost, fiddler, or thespian?

....

Picture Clue **Q6**

8 Which one of these birds does not suck nectar from flowers—crimson topaz, white-tipped sicklebill, or potoo?

....

9 Which of these is a lizard—tokay, tokkin, or tokamak?

....

10 Which of these animals lays its eggs in water—salamander, crocodile, or sea snake?

Amazing NATURE

Be a **Genius**

1 Reptiles lay their eggs in water. True or false?

....

2 Which type of reptile has a tough shell and spends much of its life at sea?

....

3 Which species is larger, the Nile crocodile or the American alligator?

....

4 What K is the world's largest lizard?

Picture Clue **Q4**

....

5 Which snake would you fear if you lived in India—king cobra or black mamba?

....

6 Which of these animals is a crocodilian—gharial, gastropod, or gar?

....

7 While boas give birth to live young, pythons lay eggs. True or false?

....

8 There is only one lizard that forages for food in the sea. Can you name it?

....

9 Which lizard is able to "walk" on water?

....

10 What T is the only remaining member of a group of reptiles that looks like a lizard, and is only found on small islands off New Zealand?

Lucky **Dip**

1 Did dinosaurs become extinct around 6.5 million years ago or 65 million years ago?

....

2 Bats can use echolocation to detect an object that is the width of a human hair. True or false?

....

3 What B is a type of fuel that is made from plants such as corn?

....

4 Where is Norway's Global Seed Vault, which contains more than 4.5 million seeds?

....

5 What G is part of a bird's body in which food is ground up?

....

6 What group of animals do octopuses belong to— arthropods, mollusks, or amphibians?

....

7 What are baby sharks called—cubs or pups?

....

8 What A is the name of a genetic mutation that causes animals to lack the pigment that colors hair and eyes?

....

9 What does a dendrochronologist count to calculate the age of a tree?

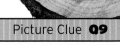

Picture Clue **09**

....

10 What name is given to someone who studies fossil animals?
a Fossilologist **b** Corpsologist **c** Paleontologist

Marine
Marvels

Some of nature's most awesome events occur beneath the surface of the sea and at its coasts. Hidden from human eyes, convoys of lobsters march across the seabed, while blooms of golden jellyfish gently propel themselves through salty waters, and colorful squid dance for their mates.

Golden jellies

Up to ten million golden jellyfish migrate in the marine lakes at Palau, in the Pacific Ocean. The saline lakes are enclosed, but still experience tidal flows because ocean water has access to them. Every morning, the jellyfish move up to the surface of the water and swim across the lake, following the course of the Sun. Sunlight is essential for the health of the algae that live inside the jellyfish and provide them with energy.

Flash dance

The Australian giant cuttlefish grows to 5 ft (1.5 m) in length. In winter, many thousands migrate to shallow waters where the males dazzle females with spectacular displays of color. The dances begin with a show of size, as the males stretch out their "arms" to prove their superiority, and zebra patterns whizz down their flanks. Like other cuttlefish, these giants can change color in an instant, and they produce a show so impressive that divers, as well as female cuttlefish, gather to enjoy the performance.

▶ Golden jellyfish bask in sunlight so that the microscopic algae that live inside them have access to the light rays they need to survive.

▲ A male broadclub cuttlefish shields his mate from a potential rival during their courtship ritual.

SPINY LOBSTERS MIGRATE UP TO 30 MI (ABOUT 50 KM) IN A FEW DAYS. BY WALKING IN SINGLE FILE THEY REDUCE DRAG, SO THEY CAN MARCH AT DOUBLE-QUICK TIME!

Quick march

Late summer storms spur Caribbean spiny lobsters into action. As their coastal waters cool, and low winds make the shallow waters murky, the lobsters get ready to move. Lined up in single file, the intrepid crustaceans march to deeper areas, where warm water speeds the development of the females' eggs. They will mate here, and return to the shallows in spring.

▲ Each spiny lobster touches the tail fan of the lobster in front as it walks, forming an orderly line. It's a bizarre event, and one that few people ever witness.

Total **Recall**

1 Which animals are famous for their flashy displays of dazzling color?

....

2 Do golden jellyfish live in the sea or saline lakes?

....

3 What C is the way that an animal impresses a possible mate?

....

4 What type of animal is a spiny lobster—a crustacean or an arachnid?

....

5 What M describes the movement of large numbers of golden jellyfish or spiny lobsters?

....

6 Do cuttlefish have shells?

....

7 What A is a tiny plant that lives inside a golden jellyfish?

....

8 Why do spiny lobsters march in single file?

....

9 In which ocean would you find the Palau Islands?

....

10 Do golden jellyfish swim toward the Sun or away from it?

Amazing NATURE

Body SCIENCE

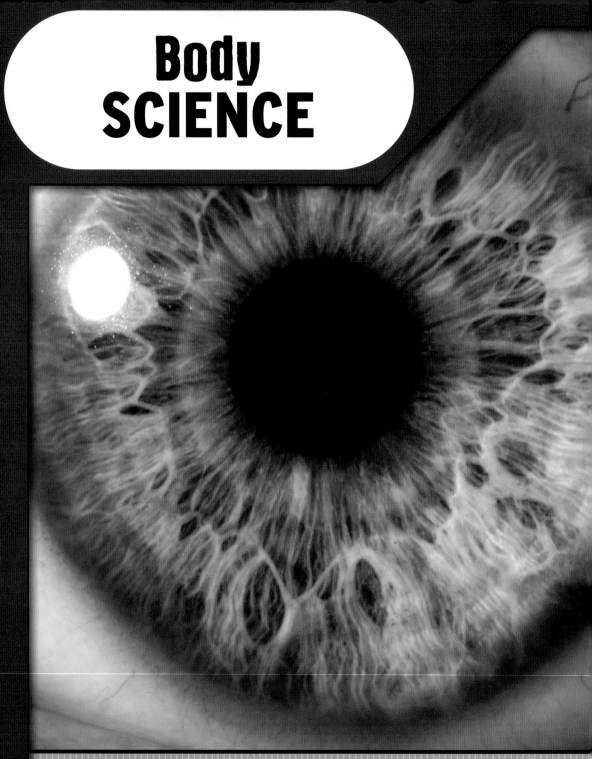

The colored part of the eye, called the iris, is a collarlike ring of two sets of muscle. These contract in opposition to alter its size.

A, B, or **C**

1 If you have cataracts, which part of your body needs medical attention?
a Eyes **b** Ears **c** Feet

2 How fast do nerve signals travel?
a Up to 6 ft/s (1.8 m/s) **b** Up to 395 ft/s (120 m/s) **c** Up to one mi/s (1.6 km/s)

3 How many chromosomes does a human sperm cell contain?
a 46 **b** 26 **c** 23

4 Where are the body's strongest muscles?
a Jaws **b** Intestines **c** Thighs

5 What name is given to the body's chemical messengers?
a Hormones **b** Enzymes **c** Erythrocytes

6 Bones are packed with living cells. What are they called?
a Highcytes **b** Osteocytes **c** Marrowblasts

7 What type of animal is a head louse?
a Spider **b** Insect **c** Crustacean

8 What word describes artificial body parts?
a Bionic **b** Biorhythmic **c** Biodegradable

9 Which hormone prepares the body for "fight or flight?"
a Testosterone **b** Prolactin **c** Adrenaline

10 The eye's retina contains rods and what else?
a Lines **b** Cones **c** Pods

Picture Clue **Q9**

Body SCIENCE

ANSWERS 1. a Eyes 2. b Up to 395 ft/s (120 m/s) 3. c 23 4. a Jaws 5. a Hormones 6. b Osteocytes 7. b Insect 8. a Bionic 9. c Adrenaline 10. b Cones

True or False?

1 The reproductive system is the only system that the body can survive without.

2 Scalp hair grows at a rate of 0.1 in (2–3 mm) a day.

3 Bone cells are the longest cells in the body, reaching up to 39 in (one m) in the human leg.

4 The mineral calcium makes up about 65 percent of the human body by mass.

5 The human body can make two million red blood cells a second.

6 Humans can control their body temperature. The temperature control system is called a hippogriff.

7 When reading, the most active areas in the brain are in the left hemisphere.

8 Humans have five main senses: sight, hearing, touch, smell, and taste.

9 Color-detecting cells in the human eye can distinguish about ten million colors.

10 When a fertilized human egg splits in two, non-identical twins will result.

ANSWERS 1. True. 2. False: it grows about 0.1 in (2–3 mm) a week. 3. False: nerve cells (neurons) are the longest cells in the body 4. False: calcium makes up just 1.5 percent of the body's mass 5. True. 6. False: it is called the hypothalamus 7. True 8. True 9. True 10. False: non-identical twins grow from two different fertilized eggs

1 Which animals were used for bloodletting, and are now used to aid the reattachment of body parts?

....

2 Which Biblical character lends his name to a part of the neck that is more obvious in men than in women?

....

3 What medical instrument is used to listen to the heart beating, or to breathing?

....

4 Which Scottish scientist discovered the effect of penicillin on bacteria?

....

5 The disease tuberculosis affects which organ?

....

6 What P is the time when a child's body matures into adulthood?

....

7 What is the name of the transparent layer at the front of the eye—cortex, cornea, or corpuscle?

....

8 Which disease is caused by a lack of Vitamin C—scurvy or rickets?

....

9 If a person is described as a universal donor, what blood group do they have?

....

10 REM is a type of sleep. What does REM stand for?

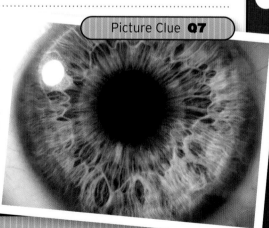

Picture Clue **Q7**

Body SCIENCE

Odd One **Out**

1 Which of these is not a human bone?
a Scapula **b** Femur **c** Aorta

2 One of these cells is not a type of white blood cell:
a Erythrocyte **b** Lymphocyte **c** Neutrophil

3 Which of these is not a genuine blood group?
a O **b** OA **c** A

4 Which scientist was not involved in the discovery of the structure of DNA?
a Joseph Lister **b** Maurice Wilkins **c** Rosalind Franklin

5 One of these is not found inside skin. Which one?
a Keratin **b** Sebum **c** Epiglottis

6 Which disease is caused by bacteria and not a virus?
a Chickenpox **b** Flu **c** Typhoid fever

7 One of these compounds does not give color to parts of the body:
a Amylase **b** Melanin **c** Hemoglobin

8 Urine contains lots of substances, but not one of these:
a Salts **b** Calcium **c** Fiber

9 Which food is a good source of iron?
a Spinach **b** Steak **c** Spaghetti

10 One of these is not an organ:
a Skin **b** Appendix **c** Brain

Picture Clue **Q8**

Body SCIENCE

Name the **Number**

1 How long does it take a toenail to grow from bottom to top—up to 6 months or up to 18 months?

....

2 How many teeth do most adults have in their mouths, including wisdom teeth?

....

3 How many separate bones make up the human skull?

....

4 How many weeks does it take for a human baby to grow, from fertilized egg to birth?

....

Picture Clue **Q4**

5 Human red blood cells are constantly replaced. How many days does each one live for (to the nearest 10)?

....

6 How many bones do adult humans have—206 or 350?

....

7 How many calories are in a medium-sized banana—40, 70, or 100?

....

8 After chewing and swallowing, how long does it take food to reach your stomach?

....

9 How many bones make up the ossicles, the tiny bones inside the ear?

....

10 How many fingerprints does the FBI in the USA currently have on its database (to the nearest ten million)?

Body SCIENCE

What am I?

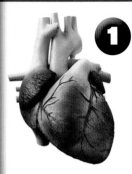

1 I pump blood around the body.

5 I carry messages from the brain to every part of the body.

2 I am part of the head and I protect the brain.

6 I am used to chew food.

3 I can be short and fine, as well as long, and I grow on the skin.

7 I am like the body's computer.

4 As part of reproduction, I fertilize the female egg cell.

8 I digest food when it is swallowed.

 **9** I clean the blood, turning waste fluid into urine.

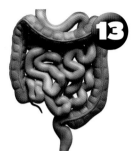 **13** I take solid waste away from the stomach.

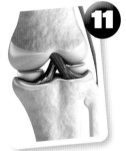 **10** I take in air and supply oxygen to the body.

 **14** I detect light and movement and send this information to the brain.

 **11** I connect the upper and lower leg.

 **15** I cover the skeleton and enable the body to move.

 **12** I collect sound and help control the body's balance.

 **16** I am a temporary storage "bag" with stretchy walls. I collect urine.

Body SCIENCE

Starting with **B**

Body SCIENCE

1 What body fluid carries oxygen and carbon dioxide around the body?

....

2 Which solid tissue is made of calcium salts and supports the body?

....

3 A very young human being is called what?

....

4 Which micro-organisms are found all over the body, and inside it?

....

5 What is the column of vertebrae that connects the skull to the pelvis called?

....

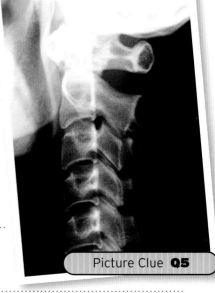

Picture Clue **Q5**

6 Sensors in your ears stop you from falling over. What is this called?

....

7 Which part of your body contains more than 100 billion nerve cells?

....

8 What is the surname of the South African surgeon who carried out the first heart transplant?

....

9 Which procedure is the removal and examination of a piece of the body, to check for signs of disease?

....

10 Bronchitis affects which part of the body?

Be a **Genius**

Body SCIENCE

1 What does the skull do?

....

2 What type of cell makes up most of the brain—lymphocyte or nerve cell?

....

3 Which blood vessels carry oxygen to the brain—arteries or veins?

....

4 Which area of the brain controls the movement of muscles in the body?

Picture Clue **Q3**

....

5 The left side of the brain controls the right side of the body. True or false?

....

6 Which part of the brain is sometimes called "gray matter?"

....

7 What are the halves of the brain called?

....

8 How much of your body's blood is used by the brain? Five, ten or 20 percent?

....

9 What sleep hormone is made by the tiny pineal gland in the center of the brain?

....

10 What B is an area in the brain that is concerned with speech?

ANSWERS 1. It protects the brain 2. Nerve cell 3. Arteries 4. Motor cortex 5. True 6. Cerebral cortex 7. Hemispheres 8. 20 percent 9. Melatonin 10. Broca's Area

What am I?

Picture Clue **Q1**

1 I am a cavity, surrounded by hairs and mucus. Sometimes, air is forced out of me at 90 mph (145 km/h).

2 I am a muscle that is covered in taste buds and helps the body to chew food.

3 I'm continually bathed in a liquid that washes away bacteria and bits of food.

4 I am exposed to the outside world, but I'm surrounded by sweat, hair, greasy sebum, and body salts.

5 I produce a hormone called insulin that helps to control the glucose levels in the body.

6 I am on a taut, stretchy membrane inside the head. Every time there is a sound, the membrane vibrates.

7 I am also known as the gullet. I take chewed food from the throat to the stomach.

8 I am in the tube that connects the mouth to the lungs, taking air in and out of the body.

9 I am made up of atriums and ventricles.

10 I am inside bone, in an area where red and white blood cells and platelets are made.

ANSWERS 1. Nose 2. Tongue 3. Mouth 4. Skin 5. Pancreas 6. Eardrum 7. Esophagus 8. Trachea 9. Heart 10. Marrow

True or **False?**

1 Skin, hair, and nails form part of the integumentary system.

2 The trachea is a tube that takes gases to and from the stomach.

3 Women have lower metabolic rates than men.

4 The tubes that carry eggs from the ovary to the womb are called fallopian tubes.

5 The common carotid artery supplies the head with oxygen-containing blood.

6 Fingerprints develop about four months after birth.

7 The body's urinary system controls water levels and removes waste products.

8 Doctors use an ophthalmoscope to examine ears.

9 CPR is a technique used to save lives. It stands for Chest Press Revive.

10 Females have two X chromosomes and males have two Y chromosomes.

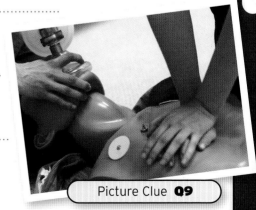

Picture Clue **Q9**

Body SCIENCE

Picture **It**

1 What D is the system that processes food in the body?

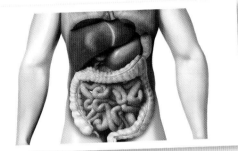

2 Is this inside a bone cell or inside a nerve cell?

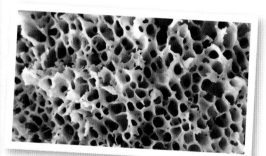

3 This mineral is found in dairy products such as cheese, and it hardens bone. What is it?

4 You have about 25 trillion of these. What are they?

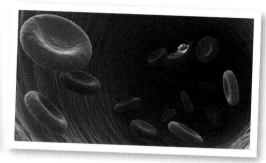

5 How many bones are in the human foot?

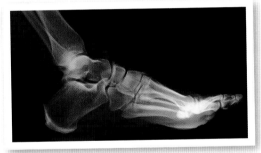

6 What P can live on, or in, the body and does it harm?

7 Which bacteria live in your gut and provide you with vitamin B1?

8 Which system defends the body against germs?

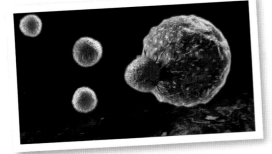

9 Which vessels carry blood to the heart?

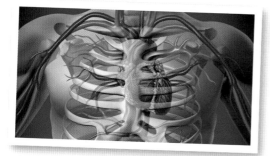

10 What is the center of a cell called?

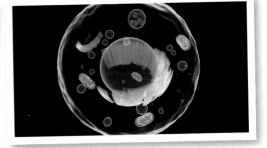

11 What S forms when the body protects a wound from infection?

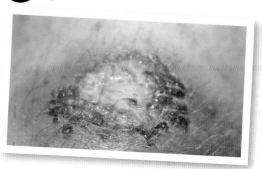

12 What is a baby called at 40 days old—fetus or embryo?

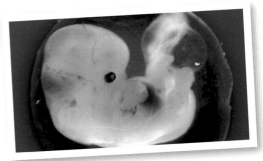

A, B, or **C**

1 Which blood vessels are the smallest?
a Veins **b** Arteries **c** Capillaries

2 Golgi bodies are found in cells. What do they process?
a Fats **b** Carbohydrates **c** Proteins

3 Where would you find the cerebral cortex?
a Brain **b** Kidney **c** Spinal column

4 Where is the organ that controls balance?
a Sternum **b** Ear **c** Liver

5 Which vitamin prevents rickets?
a E **b** D **c** C

Picture Clue **Q5**

6 Which disease did Edward Jenner help to eradicate?
a Smallpox **b** Chickenpox **c** Anthrax

7 How many chromosomes does a haploid human cell have?
a Normal amount **b** Half the normal amount **c** Double the normal amount

8 Acupuncture is an alternative therapy. What implements does it use?
a Hot rocks **b** Needles **c** Small hammers

9 In human reproduction, which develops first?
a Zygote **b** Fetus **c** Embryo

10 What is deoxyribonucleic acid better known as?
a Retinol **b** DNA **c** Cytoplasm

Starting with **H**

1 What red protein transports oxygen around the body in blood?

.... (Picture Clue **Q2**)

2 On each one of these, you have four fingers and a thumb.

....

3 These are tendons at the back of the knees.

....

4 Name a parasite that lives on the head and lays eggs that are called nits.

....

5 In 1628, which William first described how blood circulates around the body?

....

6 What type of remedy is made purely from plants?

....

7 What do the letters HIV stand for?

....

8 What name is given to the international project that decodes the DNA of Homo sapiens?

....

9 What part of the brain controls body temperature, thirst, and hunger?

....

10 From what are you suffering if you have involuntary spasms of the diaphragm?

Body SCIENCE

ANSWERS 1. Hemoglobin 2. Hand 3. Hamstrings 4. Head louse 5. Harvey 6. Herbal 7. Human Immunodeficiency Virus 8. Human Genome Project 9. Hypothalamus 10. Hiccups

Be a **Genius**

1 We have fewer hairs per area of skin than chimpanzees. True or false?

....

2 What M is the group of animals that has hair, or fur, and feeds its young with milk?

....

3 Does hair grow from a foolscap, a folly, or a follicle?

....

Picture Clue **Q2**

4 How many hairs are growing on an average human head at any one time (to the nearest 10,000)?

....

5 Which hormone causes male pattern baldness?

....

6 What M is the pigment that colors hair?

....

7 Which character from an ancient story had superhuman strength—until Delilah cut his hair?

....

8 Name the glands that produce the oil that makes hair smooth and shiny.

....

9 People with curly hair have hair follicles that are curly. True or false?

....

10 What protein is the main ingredient of hair?

Lucky Dip

1 What W is another word for uterus?

....

2 Which body tissue has a honeycomb structure that keeps it lightweight, but strong and flexible?

....

3 Which parasite may reach 30 ft (9 m) in length and can be passed on by eating undercooked food?

....

4 What type of cells might scientists use to grow new tissue—stem or root?

....

5 What verb describes the process of breathing in?

....

Picture Clue **Q7**

6 Where do female sex cells (ova) develop: ovaries or oviducts?

....

7 What clear, yellowish liquid is the basis of blood?

....

8 Artificial skin can be grown in laboratories. True or false?

....

9 What are the branching threadlike ends of nerve cells called?

....

10 Where are hormones made?
a Endocrine glands **b** Endoscope glands **c** Endotherm glands

BODY SCIENCE

MUSCLE
Power

Every move the body makes needs muscles, from lifting a finger to jumping in the air—even for sitting still. Without muscles, the body would slump like a sack of potatoes. Muscles are amazing little motors that work instantly, whenever they are needed, by constantly contracting and relaxing.

Power stripes

Muscles get their power from bundles of fibers that contract and relax. Inside each fiber are alternating, interlocking stripes or "filaments" of actin and myosin. When the brain tells a muscle to contract, little buds on each myosin filament twist, pulling on the actin filaments and making the muscle shorter. Each time a muscle contracts, another muscle fiber needs to shorten in the opposite direction to pull it back to its original length.

▶ Muscles work in pairs of actin and myosin filaments because they can only shorten themselves.

Muscle building

During exercise, the muscles grow larger. At first, the fibers simply grow fatter. With regular exercise, the body grows new muscle fibers, which means they become stronger. The blood supply improves, too, so the muscles can work longer without tiring.

▲ The body has several layers of muscle. Most are attached to bones with fibers called tendons.

THE STRONGEST MUSCLES ARE THE MASSETER MUSCLES, WHICH CONTROL THE JAW'S BITING MOVEMENT.

▶ Fibers in the voluntary muscles move the bones.

Outside and in

The body has two kinds of muscle—voluntary muscles that are under conscious control and involuntary muscles that work automatically. Voluntary muscles cover the skeleton and allow the body to move. Involuntary muscles control bodily functions, such as the heartbeat.

▲ The walls of the heart are made of cardiac muscle.

On demand

There are 640 voluntary muscles on the skeleton. The brain can only consciously control combinations that work together, rather than individuals. The longest is the sartorius muscle at the front of the thigh, while the biggest is the gluteus maximus in the buttocks.

Total **Recall**

1 What are the strongest muscles?

....

2 How many types of muscle are there?

....

3 How many voluntary muscles are on the skeleton?

....

4 What are the parts of a muscle that contract and relax?

....

5 When a muscle contracts, does it get longer or shorter?

....

6 What is the longest voluntary muscle?

....

7 What R describes a muscle that is not contracting?

....

8 Where is the biggest voluntary muscle?

....

9 Is the heart a voluntary or involuntary muscle?

....

10 What T is a tough fiber that attaches muscle to bone?

ANSWERS: 1. Masseter (jaw) muscles 2. Two: voluntary and involuntary 3. 640 4. Fibers 5. Shorter 6. Sartorius muscle 7. Relaxed 8. Buttocks 9. Involuntary 10. Tendon

Speed
MACHINES

Hydroplanes skim across the surface of the water, which uses far less energy than moving through the water. This allows the boats to travel at high speeds—up to 200 mph (320 km/h).

A, B, or C

1 Which of the following is not a type of high-speed train?
a Maglev **b** Stephenson's Rocket **c** Harmony Express

2 Aircraft that fly faster than the speed of sound are:
a Hypertonic **b** Ultrasonic **c** Supersonic

3 What is the fastest-growing type of international powerboat racing?
a Grand Prix of the Sails **b** Grand Prix of the Sea **c** Grand Prix of the Sun

4 How long does it take the Hubble Space Telescope to make one orbit of Earth?
a 97 minutes **b** 97 hours **c** 97 days

5 How many hulls does a trimaran have?
a One **b** Two **c** Three

6 What is the mechanical device with angled blades that forces a boat forward?
a Turbine **b** Cogwheel **c** Propeller

7 Which of these cyclists won the Tour de France in 2012?
a Cadel Evans **b** Bradley Wiggins **c** Mark Cavendish

8 What is the study of airflow around objects?
a Aerodynamics **b** Hydraulics **c** Phonics

9 When did helmets become compulsory for F1 drivers?
a 1953 **b** 1963 **c** 1973

10 Which of these spacecraft began the Space Race in 1957?
a Sputnik I **b** Pioneer I **c** Vostok I

Picture Clue **Q10**

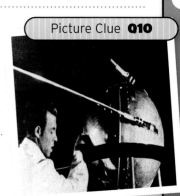

Speed MACHINES

True or **False?**

1 Some fighter planes have tiny wings on their nose, called mallards.

....

2 The formula for calculating speed is distance × time.

....

3 Some of the fastest aircraft are unable to takeoff under their own power.

....

4 The International Space Station orbits Earth so fast that astronauts onboard see 15 sunrises in ever 24 hours.

....

5 The course record for the Oxford–Cambridge Boat Race is under 17 minutes.

....

6 100 mi is equivalent to approximately 120 km.

....

7 When the Bugatti Veyron reaches 140 mph (220 km/h) it automatically lowers itself closer to the ground.

....

8 Sound travels faster in warm air than in cold air.

....

Picture Clue **09**

9 F1 cars are faster than IndyCars in a straight line.

....

10 The catapults that launch navy planes from aircraft carriers are powered by nuclear energy.

Lucky **Dip**

1 A GPS satellite orbit is how much higher than that of the International Space Station—6, 60, or 600?

2 What term is used to describe the speed that data transfers from the Internet to a computer?

3 Is the world record yacht speed higher or lower than 60 mph (96.6 km/h)?

4 How many classes of Grand Prix of the Sea (GPS) boats are there?

Picture Clue **Q6**

5 Which of these vehicles has not broken a speed record—Lockheed SR-71 Blackbird, *Bluebird K7*, or White Knight?

6 What is faster—the speed of sound or the speed of light?

7 What type of vehicle is a velocipede?

8 Sound travels faster through a vacuum than in air. True or false?

9 To set an official airspeed record, planes must have air-breathing engines. True or false?

10 What is the approximate speed of light?
a 116,000 mi/sec (186,000 km/sec) **b** 186,000 mi/sec (300,000 km/sec)
c 300,000 mi/sec (483,000 km/sec)

Odd One **Out**

1 Which of these safety devices is not carried on a Formula 1 car: fire extinguisher system, survival cell, or parachute?

....

2 Who is the current holder of the world water speed record: Ken Warby, Andy Green, or Major George T. Morgan?

....

3 Which of these is not a supercomputer: Tianhe-1A, TOP500, or K?

....

4 The Space Shuttle's heat shield tiles are made of what—silica and air, silica and titanium, or silica and carbon fiber?

....

5 Which of these Formula 1 drivers has never driven for McLaren: Nigel Mansell, Lewis Hamilton, or Michael Schumacher?

....

6 Which of these vehicles takes less than one second to accelerate to 60 mph (100 km/h): Formula 1 car, dragster, or Suzuki Hayabusa motorbike?

....

7 Which of these things will not improve aerodynamics: more drag, streamlined shape, or reduced friction?

....

8 Which animal inspired the creators of high-tech swimsuits for athletes: shark, tuna, or dolphin?

....

9 When did *Hydroptère* set a world record yacht speed: 2009, 2010, or 2011?

....

10 Which feature did Penny Farthing bicycles lack— brakes, saddle, or chain?

Picture Clue **Q10**

Name the **Number**

1 How many times did Michael Schumacher hold pole position in Formula 1, between 1994 and 2006?

....

2 How many people are needed to crew GPS boats—at least 2, 3, or 4?

....

3 The Space Shuttle Orbiter is covered with more than 24,000 or 240,000 tiles?

....

4 What was Concorde's top speed—1,300 mph (2,100 km/h) or 1,700 mph (2,735 km/h)?

....

5 What is the jet-powered water speed record (to the nearest 10 km/h)?

....

6 The first supercomputer was built in 1964. How many calculations could it do in one second?

....

7 How many motocross world titles did Stefan Everts of Belgium win between 1991 and 2006?

....

8 If a vessel travels at a speed of one nautical mile an hour, how many knots is it traveling at?

....

9 Concorde first flew in 1969. In what year was it retired?

....

10 In what year did the first official Paralympic Games take place, in Rome?

Speed MACHINES

Picture Clue **Q9**

What am I?

1
I am a type of train with no wheels. I don't touch the track.

2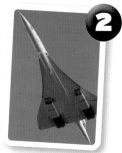
I am a supersonic plane and broke many records. I am now retired.

3
We perform stunning aerobatic displays.

4
I am a partly reusable spacecraft. I was part of a space exploration programme for 30 years.

5
I am made of carbon fiber. I am used on a smooth, curved track. I have no brakes.

6
I was built in 1938. I am the world's fastest steam train.

7
I am built to be as light and fast as possible. My engine is behind my driver.

8
I have two wheels and am ridden in the MotoGP championship.

9 I was the world's first artificial satellite. I was launched in 1957.

13 I set the world record for an aircraft powered by a jet engine.

10 I transported the first men to land on the Moon in 1969.

14 I am the fastest wooden rollercoaster in the world. You can find me in New Jersey, U.S.

11 I broke the Outright World Speed Sailing Record in 2012.

15 I am a supercar that can reach speeds of 250 mph (400 km/h). I cost over $2 million (£1.5 million).

12 I have three wheels. You would see me in the Paralympic Games.

16 My wings cover enough space to park 140 cars. I am the world's biggest airliner.

Speed MACHINES

Starting with T

1 What metal with the atomic number 22 can withstand huge temperatures and is used in the manufacture of aircraft and spacecraft?

....

2 What word describes a driving, or pushing, force that was also used to name a land-speed record car?

....

3 TGVs are the world's fastest conventional trains. What do the letters TGV stand for?

....

4 Which city is home to the world's busiest underground railway network?

....

Picture Clue **Q4**

5 What "TV" is the constant speed that a falling object reaches when air resistance prevents further acceleration?

....

6 What T is a mechanical device that controls the flow of fuel or power to an engine?

....

7 Ayrton Senna died in the 1994 San Marino Grand Prix. What was the name of the notorious curve he was exiting as he crashed?

....

8 How many cylinders does a Dodge Viper engine have?

....

9 What T means changing the direction of a sailing ship?

....

10 To protect its aluminum structure, the Space Shuttle Orbiter was covered with what heat-resistant objects?

Be a **Genius**

1 What is a plane's black box—its flight recorder or altitude meter?

....

2 What type of plane engine gets its name from the French word *jeter*, which means to throw?

....

3 What structure with curved surfaces helps a plane to fly—aerofoil, aerobic, or aerosol?

....

4 What name is given to planes that are used to show a pilot's great skill and daring in aerobatic displays?

Picture Clue **Q4**

....

5 What is the name of the force that slows down an aircraft?

....

6 When a plane flies at Mach 1, is it flying at the speed of sound or the speed of light?

....

7 Does downforce decrease or increase maneuverability?

....

8 What was the name of the plane that Charles Lindbergh flew on the first non-stop solo flight from New York to Paris in 1927?

....

9 Who was the first woman to fly solo from England to Australia?

....

10 What was the name of the first plane to fly faster than sound?

Speed MACHINES

Who am I?

1 I am the fighter pilot who drove *Thrust SSC* on its record-smashing run.

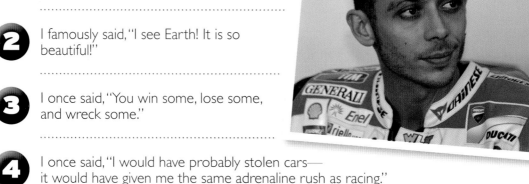

Picture Clue **Q4**

2 I famously said, "I see Earth! It is so beautiful!"

3 I once said, "You win some, lose some, and wreck some."

4 I once said, "I would have probably stolen cars— it would have given me the same adrenaline rush as racing."

5 I made history in 1947 by piloting the rocket-powered X-1 through the sound barrier.

6 I once said, "When you are fitted in a racing car and you race to win, second or third place is not enough."

7 I am the only person ever to set new land speed and water speed records in the same year—1964.

8 I once said, "The 317.60 mph, though important, was only the icing on a wonderful cake."

9 I studied the effects of g-force on the human body in the 1940s and '50s by strapping myself to a rocket sled.

10 I set a land speed record in 1983, in a jet-powered car.

ANSWERS 1. Andy Green 2. Yuri Gagarin 3. Dale Earnhardt 4. Valentino Rossi 5. Chuck Yeager 6. Ayrton Senna 7. Donald Campbell 8. Ken Warby 9. Dr. John Stapp 10. Richard Noble

True or **False?**

1 French high-speed TGV trains are the fastest passenger trains in service in the world.

....

2 Sonic booms can be heard from boats.

....

3 The Blackbird spy-plane could fly at more than three times the speed of sound.

....

4 The three astronauts in *Apollo 10*'s command module traveled faster than any human traveled before, or since.

....

5 International Butterflies are small one-person sailing boats that have underwater wings.

....

6 Record-breaking car *Spirit of America* was powered by an engine from an old jet fighter plane.

....

7 Carbon fiber is much lighter than steel, but is twice as strong.

....

8 NASCAR is an acronym for the National Association for Sports Cars and Racing.

....

9 The heat shield of a spacecraft entering the Martian atmosphere is hot enough to melt gold.

....

10 A computer's processing power is measured in gigapops.

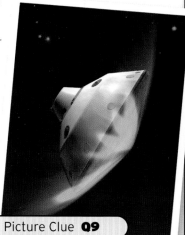

Picture Clue **Q9**

Speed MACHINES

Picture It

1 What does the vapor cone around this plane mean?

2 Name this space telescope, which launched in 1990.

3 This satellite is a Meteosat. Does it monitor weather or traffic?

4 What small boat has a helicopter engine and skims the water's surface?

5 What force has this rider overcome to rise up the wall?

6 What type of helicopter is this, also the name of a wild cat?

7 What is this type of train?

8 What was the name of Andy Green's record-breaking jet-car?

9 Which sports car produced by Lamborghini is named after a breed of fighting bull?

10 Where did the Helios space probes travel to in 1974 and 1976?

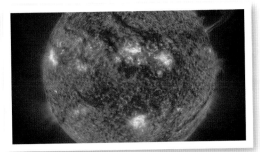

11 Is this car called a dragoon or a dragster?

12 In which U.S. state is Black Rock Desert, where *Thrust* SSC broke the land speed record?

A, B, or C

1 Which of these words is not a synonym for "quick?"
a Expeditious **b** Whirlwind **c** Protracted

2 Which vehicles take part in the Road Racing World Championship Grand Prix?
a Tricycles **b** Solar-powered cars **c** Motorcycles

3 In what year did the Space Shuttle Atlantis blast off on its final journey?
a 2010 **b** 2011 **c** 2012

4 Which of these does not travel at the speed of light?
a Seismic waves from an earthquake **b** Microwaves **c** Gamma rays

5 What are high performance motorcycles called?
a Megabikes **b** Ultrabikes **c** Superbikes

Picture Clue **Q5**

6 What is the world's fastest pick-up truck called?
a *Flash Dance* **b** *Flash Light* **c** *Flash Fire*

7 Which vehicle is the world's fastest supercar?
a SSC Ultimate Aero **b** Bugatti Veyron **c** Pontiac PGO

8 What term describes the data transfer from a computer to the Internet?
a Upload speed **b** Mashup speed **c** Download speed

9 What did IBM's Deep Blue supercomputer win in 1996?
a Chess match **b** Tennis game **c** Car racing game

10 What speed must a rocket reach to blast away from Earth into space?
a 15,000 mph (24,000 km/h) **b** 20,000 mph (32,300 km/h)
c 25,000 mph (40,300 km/h)

Odd One **Out**

1 Which of these features would not be found on a plane—spoiler, aileron, or fusilli?

....

2 Which of these is not a type of bicycle—velocipede, clunker, or pedalo?

....

Picture Clue **Q4**

3 Which country does not have one of the top three longest rail networks in the world—Russia, USA, or Brazil?

....

4 Which of these countries has not yet developed a high-speed train—France, Japan, or Australia?

....

5 Which of these is not a term used to describe part of a boat—starport, aft, or forward?

....

6 General Motors, Honda, or Toyota—which car manufacturer is not one of the world's top five (measured in number of cars made)?

....

7 Which of these actions can be performed by a helicopter, but not by a plane—fly backward, fly upside down, or carry missiles?

....

8 Which spacecraft zoomed close to the Sun for a scientific study—Helios I, Pioneer 10, or Mariner 9?

....

9 Which of these is not an ocean liner—MS *Oasis of the Seas*, SS *United States*, or HMS *Trafalgar*?

....

10 Which of these vehicles is both a plane and a car—the Terrafugia Transition, the Steamin' Demon, or the Peel P50?

Speed MACHINES

Be a **Genius**

1 Which of these is not a fossil fuel: coal, gas, oil, or wind?

Picture Clue **Q1**

2 Cars taking part if the World Solar Challenge are powered by what?

3 What is the name of the rubbing force that slows down moving things?

4 Which of these is not a type of car: coupé, limousine, harrier, saloon, or hatchback?

5 An airplane must take off when it reaches its V1 speed. What speed must it reach to be able to climb safely—V2 or V3?

6 An engine is a machine that converts energy into magnetic motion. True or false?

7 Who was granted a patent for the internal combustion engine in 1879 and built the first gasoline (petrol) powered cars?

8 Approximately how many new cars are built every year worldwide (to the nearest five million)?

9 Which spy plane set the world air-speed record in 1976, with a speed of 2,193 mph (3,529 km/h)?

10 What name was given to a concept car developed by Ford in the 1950s, designed to run on nuclear fuel?

ANSWERS 1. Wind 2. Sunlight 3. Friction 4. Harrier 5. V2 6. False: it converts energy into mechanical motion 7. Karl Benz 8. 60 million 9. The Lockheed SR-71 Blackbird 10. Ford Nucleon (it was never built)

Lucky **Dip**

1 What stops a passenger falling out of a rollercoaster?
a Inert gases **b** Tertiary forces **c** Inertia

2 What C is a lever that is used to throw things?

3 The crack of a whip is a tiny sonic boom. The boom is created because hydrogen molecules are squashed together. True or false?

4 How many Concorde aircraft were in service, carrying more than 2.5 million people from 1976 until its retirement?

5 Formula 1 cars can be driven so fast that they could, in theory, be driven upside down on a ceiling. True or false?

6 An SUV is a high-performance, four-wheel-drive car. What do the letters SUV stand for?

7 Which explosive gas with atomic number 1 is used to make fuel cells for cars?

8 What piece of equipment might an engineer use to study the forces of circular motion—a gyroscope or a gyromagnet?

9 The fastest steel rollercoaster in the world is in Dubai. What is it called?

10 The first land speed record was set in 1898 in an electric car. True or false?

ANSWERS 1. c Inertia 2. Catapult 3. False: it happens because the tip of the whip travels faster than the speed of sound. 4. 14 5. True 6. Sports Utility Vehicle 7. Hydrogen 8. Gyroscope 9. Formula Rossa 10. True

Top TAKEOFF

Planes are able to take off only if they move through the air fast enough. An airliner has to accelerate to at least 150 mph (240 km/h) before its wings create enough lift to cause the plane to defy gravity and leave the ground.

▶ Concorde's mighty jet engines powered the plane to a top speed of more than 1,300 mph (2,100 km/h).

The need for speed

The supersonic airliner Concorde had to go much faster than other airliners before it could take off. Its wings were built for flying at twice the speed of sound, so they didn't produce much lift at lower speeds. Concorde had to reach 225 mph (360 km/h) before its slender wings generated enough upward force for takeoff.

GIANT flyer

The enormous Airbus A380 is the world's biggest airliner. Its massive wings cover enough space to park 140 cars. This huge airliner accelerates to a speed of 170 mph (280km/h) on the ground before its wings are able lift the 1.25-million-lb (625-ton) aircraft into the air.

▼ The shape and enormous size of the A380 airliner's wings enable it to take off at the same speed as much smaller, lighter planes.

THE AIRBUS A380 WEIGHS AS MUCH AS 165 ELEPHANTS.

▼ A navy pilot prepares to be launched along the deck and into the air by catapult.

Elastic fantastic

An aircraft carrier has a runway, but it isn't long enough for modern fighter jets to reach takeoff speed. Jets have to be hurled along the deck by a powerful catapult so they're going fast enough to fly when they reach the end. The catapult can boost a 47,000-lb (21-ton) plane from zero to 165 mph (265 km/h) in only two seconds.

Total **Recall**

1 What is the name of the world's biggest airliner?

....

2 Was Concorde hypertonic, hypersonic, or supersonic?

....

3 How many elephants weigh the same as the Airbus A380?

....

4 What A describes an increase in speed that a plane achieves before takeoff?

....

5 An Airbus A380 has to reach a speed of 633 mph (1,018 km/h) before it can take off. True or false?

....

6 Did Concorde fly faster or slower than the speed of sound?

....

7 Were Concorde's wings the best shape for speed or takeoff?

....

8 What L describes the upward movement of a plane—lift or lever?

....

9 Concorde's top speed was less than 1,300 mph (2,100 km/h). True or false?

....

10 How many cars could be parked in the space covered by the wings of an Airbus A380?

ANSWERS 1. Airbus A380 2. Supersonic 3. 165 4. Acceleration 5. False: it reaches a speed of 170 mph (280 km/h) 6. Faster 7. Speed 8. Lift 9. False: its top speed was more than 1,300 mph (2,100 km/h) 10. 140

Thrill
SEEKERS

Base jumping involves launching yourself off a Building, Antenna, Span (bridge), or Earth (cliff). Some jumpers wear wingsuits to provide lift when jumping from such a low altitude.

A, B, or C

1 In what aquatic sport does Tanya Streeter hold a world record?
a Ice diving **b** Cliff diving **c** Freediving

2 What valuable objects might divers find in oyster shells?
a Pearls **b** Diamonds **c** Corals

3 Chay Blyth circumnavigated the world in 1971. How long did it take?
a 292 days **b** 922 days **c** 229 days

4 Who might experience a "silt out," when visibility can fall to zero?
a Parachutist **b** Fire-eater **c** Cave diver

5 How long did Harry Houdini's career last?
a 5 years **b** 35 years **c** 55 years

6 Which human-powered vehicle travels fastest?
a Luge **b** Recumbent bike **c** Mountain bike

7 What is the most dangerous sport for women?
a Cheerleading **b** Swimming **c** Soccer

8 What might a climber attach to his boots?
a Crampons **b** Crankpins **c** Camshafts

9 What type of animal would a falconer train?
a Big cat **b** Bird of prey **c** Snake

10 In which field do pyrotechnics experts specialize?
a Flight and falling **b** Fire and fireworks **c** Speed driving

Picture Clue **Q8**

Thrill SEEKERS

True or **False?**

1 Freefall skydiving is the world's most dangerous sport, resulting in one death for every 60 jumps.

2 Fire-eaters do not use real fire, relying on fake flames created from inhaling chilli gases instead.

3 Cliff divers adopt a ball-like body shape to avoid injury when they enter the water.

Picture Clue **Q2**

4 Mountain climbers call heights above 26,000 ft (8,000 m) the Death Zone because the air is too thin to breathe.

5 The leotard is a one-piece garment made famous by a French acrobat called Jules Léotard.

6 Scientists have been unable to design a plane that can be flown using just human movement.

7 Explorers who venture into caves are known as spelunkers.

8 Sailors that want to circumnavigate the world sail eastward for an easier journey.

9 Skilled actors who take the place of movie stars when a part calls for dangerous actions are called crash dummies.

10 Snowboarders often practice their moves using roller skates and unicycles.

Thrill SEEKERS

ANSWERS 1. False: base jumping is the most dangerous sport, with one death in every 60 jumps ending in death 2. False: they use real fire 3. False: they adopt a torpedo-like pose to avoid injury 4. True 5. True 6. False 7. True 8. True: sailing westward means sailing into the wind 9. False: they are stuntmen and stuntwomen course in 1977 7. True 8. True: sailing westward means sailing into the wind 9. False: they are stuntmen and stuntwomen 10. False: they sometimes practice with skateboards though

Lucky **Dip**

1 Which female aviator disappeared while attempting to fly around the world in 1937?

....

2 Ice hockey is a thrilling game played between two teams of six players. What do they hit—a puck, a snitch, or a chuck?

....

3 Steve Fossett became the first person to circle the globe alone in a balloon. In what year did he disappear while on a short flight?

....

4 In which sport might players make a scrum?

....

5 How many players are in a soccer team?

....

6 Who is heaviest, a featherweight boxer or a bantamweight boxer?

....

7 Who invented the jet engine—Frank Whittle or Fred Whippet?

....

8 What name is given to an aerial battle between the pilots of two fighter planes?

....

9 In 2012, Felix Baumgartner skydived 24 mi (39 km). How long did his descent take—10 minutes or 10 hours?

....

10 What animal is essential for an athlete who wants to take part in equestrian events?

Picture Clue **Q10**

Thrill SEEKERS

Odd One **Out**

1 Which of these does not hold a genuine world record—fastest lawnmower, fastest crawl on hands and feet, or highest geyser surfer?

....

2 Which of these men has never been an escape artist—David Blaine, Harry Houdini, or Mo Farah?

....

3 Which of these men never went to the Antarctic—Robert Falcon Scott or David Livingstone?

....

4 Street luge, parquet, parkour—one of these is not a street sport. Which one?

....

5 Which of these is a genuine thrill sport—reverse bungee jumping, reverse skydiving, or reverse snowboarding?

....

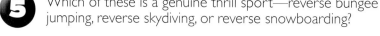

Picture Clue **Q2**

6 What would not be a good way to achieve zero gravity—travel to the center of Earth, orbit Earth in a spacecraft, or travel on a rollercoaster?

....

7 Which of these is not a stunt performed with airplanes—barnstorming, brainstorming, or wing-walking?

....

8 Which one of these has not been carried out at an altitude above 19,700 ft (6,000 m)—a dinner party, bungee jump, or free-diving?

....

9 Which of these is a genuine sport for thrill seekers—underwater cycling, whale chasing, or lava swimming?

....

10 Which of these is not a type of ski piste—red, black, or yellow?

ANSWERS 1. Highest geyser surfer. 2. Mo Farah. 3. David Livingstone. 4. Parquet—it is a type of flooring. 5. Reverse bungee jumping 6. Travel on a rollercoaster—although there are plans to make a zero gravity one! 7. Brainstorming. 8. Free-diving. 9. Underwater cycling 10. Yellow.

Name the **Number**

1 A famous boxing match between George Foreman and Muhammad Ali was called The Rumble in the Jungle. In what year did it take place?

....

2 How long did it take French sailor Jean Luc Van Den Heede to sail single-handedly westward around the world in 2004?

....

3 What speed do ski jumpers reach before taking off into the air— 60 mph (100 km/h) or 100 mph (160 km/h)?

....

4 The force of gravity is measured in gs. At how many gs would a stunt pilot lose consciousness?

....

5 In what year was escapologist Harry Houdini punched before he could prepare himself for the blows, causing a fatal infection from a ruptured appendix?

....

6 Swiss "Jetman" Yves Rossy fitted engines to his wingsuit and flew across the English Channel in 2008. How long did it take him—13 or 30 minutes?

....

7 Tillman, an English bulldog, set a world record time for a dog traveling 330 ft (100 m) on a skateboard in 2009. What was his time—9.7 or 19.7 seconds?

....

8 In 2011, how many torches was fire-eater Hubertus Wawra able to extinguish in 30 seconds?

....

9 The smallest roadworthy car is called Wind Up. How high is it?

....

10 In 2010, Jackie Bibby, the Texas Snake Man, kept 150 rattlesnakes in his sleeping bag. How long did he keep them there for—10 or 30 seconds?

What am I?

1 We work together to make shapes in the air.

2 I walk quickly to avoid burns.

3 I eat flaming objects.

4 I leap from rocky structures, with water to break my fall.

5 I have to be a strong swimmer, and be able to hold my breath.

6 I jump from different types of fixed objects, using a parachute.

7 I brave the cold to reach the top of an obstacle.

8 I often perform in a circus. I jump and swing to my catcher.

9 I perform on a thin wire at great heights.

13 I travel down snowy slopes with long, narrow strips of flexible material attached to my feet.

10 I race in a small and very fast sled, down an icy track.

14 I walk along the wing of a plane during flight.

11 I race on the back of a four-legged animal.

15 I use vaults, flips, and spins to move between obstacles.

12 I explore a subterranean world.

16 I use an adapted skateboard to hurtle downhill on the tarmac.

ANSWERS: 1. Formation skydivers 2. Fire-eater 3. Fire walker 4. Cliff diver 5. Freediver 6. Base jumper 7. Ice climber 8. Flying trapeze artist 9. High-wire artist 10. Luge racer 11. Jockey 12. Caver 13. Skier 14. Wing-walker 15. Free-runner or parkour 16. Street luge racer

Starting with S

1 What S is a board that looks like a short, broad ski and is used for sliding downhill on snow?

....

2 Performing an action that shows extreme skill and daring is known as what?

....

3 What S is used by thrill seekers to ride the crest of a wave?

....

4 What S describes how fast something is going in mph or km/h?

....

5 What desert-living invertebrate is closely related to spiders, has a venomous sting in its tail, and features in some thrill seekers' world record attempts?

....

6 What S describes a tourist who plans to leave Earth's atmosphere for pleasure or leisure?

....

7 Which desert is the location for the infamous Marathon des Sables, a six-day ultra-marathon?

....

8 What S is a type of spacecraft, such as the Challenger, used by NASA from 1981 to 2011?

....

9 Which sport involves throwing a metal ball as far as possible?

....

10 What S describes a thrill seeker who attempts his sports or adventures alone?

ANSWERS 1. Snowboard 2. Stunt 3. Surfboard 4. Speed 5. Scorpion 6. Space tourist 7. Sahara 8. Shuttle 9. Shotput 10. Solo

Be a **Genius**

1 How many pilots fly in the Red Arrows?

....

2 You have vertigo. Which adventure sport should you avoid—kayaking, scuba diving, or rock climbing?

....

3 Trapeze artists hurtle through the air at speeds of 16 mph (26 km/h) or 60 mph (100 km/h)?

....

Picture Clue **Q4**

4 Which of these men did not set a land speed record in a car—Henry Segrave, Buzz Aldrin, or Donald Campbell?

....

5 Who directed *127 Hours*, the 2010 film about a mountain climber who had to amputate his own arm when he got trapped in rocks?

....

6 How many grades of difficulty are recognized in white water rafting?

....

7 Hang gliders sometimes take on extra weight when the wind is strong. What is this weight called?

....

8 What motorsport event is the largest single-day sporting event in the world?

....

9 In 2012, a Hawaiian surfer broke the world record when he caught a mammoth wave. How tall was the wave?

....

10 How many vertical skydivers broke the world record in 2012, in Illinois, USA, with a snowflake formation (to the nearest 5)?

Thrill SEEKERS

ANSWERS 1. 9 2. Rock climbing 3. 60 mph (100 km/h) 4. Buzz Aldrin (he was an astronaut) 5. Danny Boyle 6. Six 7. Ballast 8. The Indianapolis 500 9. 78 ft (24 m) 10. 140

Where am I?

1 I am a master of Sumo, and practice this thrilling sport in the country of its origin.

2 I am exploring Krubera Cave, 7,200 ft (2,200 m) below the surface. Which mountain range am I in?

3 I am about to begin the Vendée Globe sailing race. What country am I in?

Picture Clue **Q1**

4 I am in a submarine, exploring far below the sea in the world's deepest place.

5 I am about to climb the most famous vertical rock formation, El Capitan, in the U.S. Which park am I in?

6 I am watching fire walkers at the Jia Chai festival in Phuket. What country am I in?

7 I am climbing to the summit of the world's second tallest mountain. It is said to be more dangerous than Everest.

8 I am watching pyroclastic explosions, ash bombs, and lava flows. Which type of geographical feature am I standing next to?

9 I am on the Bering Glacier, the largest glacier in the world after the Antarctic and Greenland ice sheets. What continent am I on?

10 I am in the place reached by explorer Roald Amundsen in 1911.

Thrill SEEKERS

True or **False?**

1 Blowfish brains are used to make fugu, a Japanese delicacy, but one bite of the fish's flesh causes instant death.

2 Scared people turn paler.

3 American cyclist Lance Armstrong was stripped of his many wins in 2012, following allegations of cheating.

4 On the Pacific island of Vanuatu, men tie vines to each ankle and leap off a tower to demonstrate courage and impress girls.

5 In 2009, Manjit Singh pulled a bus using his hair.

6 When a stuntman crashes a car, the crumple zone at the front of the vehicle helps to slow it down.

7 Some people in Namibia eat bullfrogs, even though their toxic skin can cause kidney failure.

8 Rope-walking was invented in China and is the most ancient form of altitude acrobatics.

9 The eyes of someone who is scared have smaller pupils than those of someone who is relaxed.

10 A parachute slows down the motion of an object using drag.

Thrill SEEKERS

ANSWERS 1. False: the internal organs and skin contain deadly poison, but the flesh is used to make fugu 2. True 3. True 4. True 5. True 6. False: it helps to absorb the impact 7. True 8. True 9. False: scared people have bigger pupils 10. True

Picture **It**

 1 What name describes parachutists —skydivers or skyfallers?

 2 Who is the tightrope walker who crossed Niagara Falls?

3 What is the name of the first successful powered aircraft, made by the Wright Brothers?

 4 Name this extreme sport.

5 What sport do the San Diego Chargers play?

6 In 1973, Phillipe Petit completed a famous high-wire walk in which U.S. city?

7 Which Russian cosmonaut was the first person in space?

8 What is the name of this daring winter sport?

9 Name this famous escapologist who died in 1926.

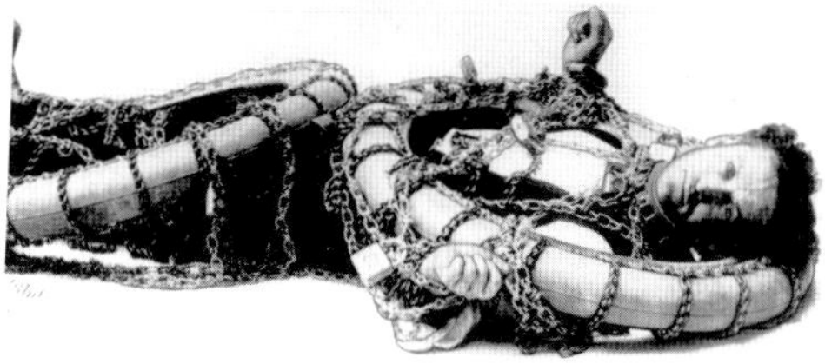

10 Which escapologist was chained to a gyroscope in 2006?

11 When did climbers first reach the summit of K2—1954 or 1964?

12 In which geographical feature did climber Aron Ralston become trapped in 2003?

ANSWERS 1. Skydivers 2. Charles Blondin 3. Wright Flyer 4. Bungee jumping 5. NFL (National Football League) 6. New York 7. Yuri Gagarin 8. Ski-jumping 9. Harry Houdini 10. David Blaine 11. 1954 12. Canyon

Be a **Genius**

1 America was named after explorer Amerigo Vespucci. True or false?

....

2 Was Jacques Cousteau a marine, Arctic, or space explorer?

....

3 Which Italian explorer sailed across the Atlantic Ocean in 1492, searching for India and found the American continent instead?

....

4 Who was the first person to reach the South Pole in 1911?

....

5 What nationality was Vasco da Gama?

....

6 Who was the second man to walk on the Moon in 1969?

....

7 It is possible that Leif Erikkson was the first European to reach the Americas. What country did he depart from—Norway or Greenland?

....

8 Which British explorer and astronomer sailed to Tahiti to observe Venus move between Earth and the Sun?

....

9 Who was the first African-American woman in space?

....

10 Which explorer named the Pacific Ocean?

Where am I?

1 I am standing at the top of a 400-ft (120-m) drop at the Holmenkollen Ski Arena.

2 This famous football stadium is home to both Milan and AC Milan.

3 I am in a 91,000-capacity stadium, which saw the thrills and drama of the 2008 Olympic Games.

4 The narrow streets of this small city make the Monaco Grand Prix one of the most exciting events in the Formula 1 calendar.

5 This American venue is the home of iconic indoor sports events.

6 This Roman stadium witnessed the deaths of an estimated 500,000 people.

7 In 2009, Usain Bolt ran 100 m in 9.58 seconds. What country was he in?

Picture Clue **Q5**

8 Roz Savage rowed across this ocean single-handedly in 2010.

9 The legendary Babe Ruth played at this baseball stadium in New York, and it has recently been rebuilt and modernized.

10 I am at the venue for the FA Cup final. The twin towers are gone, but this remains one of the most famous soccer grounds in the world.

Thrill SEEKERS

Lucky **Dip**

Thrill SEEKERS

1 What is the name of the hormone that is released when people are thrilled?

....

2 When a person is excited or scared, their heart races and their digestion slows down. True or false?

....

3 What is the normal depth limit for a scuba diver breathing air—82 ft (25 m) or 164 ft (50 m)?

....

4 Who reached the summit of Mount Everest in 1953?

....

5 How long would an astronaut stay conscious if exposed to the vacuum of space?

....

6 What is the luge speed world record?

....

7 Who achieved the highest ascent in a hot air balloon, reaching 32,500 ft (9,906 m) in January 2007?

....

8 In 2005, who set a record for the fastest solo non-stop voyage around the world, taking 71 days?

....

9 Some people eat strange objects, such as lightbulbs, bicycles, and aircraft. True or false?

....

10 What were the first names of the famous Wright brothers who flew for 12 seconds in 1903?

ANSWERS 1. Adrenalin 2. True 3. 164 ft (50 m) 4. Sir Edmund Hillary and Tenzing Norgay 5. 15 seconds 6. 86.93 mph (139.9 km/h) set by Tony Benshoof 7. David Hempleman-Adams 8. Ellen MacArthur 9. True 10. Orville and Wilbur

Be a **Genius**

1 A trophy cup is also known as a chalice. True or false?

....

2 In which city are the Taurus World Stunt Awards held each year?

....

3 In which sport is the America's Cup awarded?

....

4 How much money did David Walliams raise when he swam the English Channel in 2006?

....

Picture Clue **Q3**

5 Is the Borg-Warner trophy awarded to the Daytona 500 champion or the Indianapolis champion?

....

6 How much money does the winner of the Dubai World Cup night horse race receive—$1 million or $10 million?

....

7 Which trophy is awarded to the winner of The Rugby World Cup and is named after the game's young instigator?

....

8 In soccer, what trophy is given to the winning team of the world's most widely viewed and followed single-sport event?

....

9 What is the name of the championship trophy awarded annually to the National Hockey League—the Steren Cup or the Stanley Cup?

....

10 In ancient Greece, Olympic winners did not receive medals, but a simple wreath. What plant was the wreath made from?

Thrill SEEKERS

ANSWERS 1. True 2. Los Angeles 3. Yacht racing 4. £1 million ($1.5 million) 5. Indianapolis 500 6. $10 million (£6.2 million) 7. The William Webb Ellis Cup 8. The FIFA World Cup 9. Stanley Cup 10. Laurel

BEASTLY
Beasts

People have lived, worked, and played with wild animals for more than 30,000 years. For most of this time, the beasts got a raw deal, mostly as entertainment for humans. Now that animals in the wild are vanishing fast, we take better care of our savage friends—but interaction with potentially lethal creatures demands extreme caution.

◄ This scuba-diving cameraman is taking a grave risk. Tiger sharks are second only to great whites in their record for attacks on humans.

Making friends with Jaws

Long persecuted as killers, sharks are now getting the scientific attention they deserve. They need it—numbers are falling and up to half of all shark species are endangered. Of some 380 shark species, just four are known to attack humans. Scientists study these cautiously. Armored suits protect against a friendly nibble, but when Jaws is big—and hungry—only a cage will do.

Pooch or pack?

British wolf researcher Shaun Ellis has an unconventional approach to studying wolves. To learn about these notorious and misunderstood wild dogs he joined—and led—a wolf pack in Idaho, U.S., learning to live, hunt, eat, and howl just like them. Today he uses his knowledge to help wolves and humans live in harmony in areas where packs' territories are close to people's homes.

Swooping hunters

In medieval Europe, falconry was considered the noblest of the hunting arts. The more noble the nobleman, the bigger the bird that perched on his gloved fist. This must make today's Kazakhstan hunters the royalty of falconers, for they hunt with the world's biggest raptors—golden eagles. These powerful birds weigh as much as a small turkey, and have a 7 ft (2 m) wingspan.

▼ Thick gloves protect a Kazakhstani falconer's outstretched arms from the sharp talons of his beloved eagle.

► At his refuge in Devon, U.K., Shaun Ellis combines research with a TV program to educate the public about wolves and their behavior.

Total **Recall**

1 What S describes animals that need to be studied from the safety of a cage?

....

2 Which raptors do Kazakhstani falconers use ?

....

3 Which sharks are best known for attacking humans?

....

4 Falconry was once considered a noble hunting art. True or false?

....

5 Wolf researcher Shaun Ellis lived with wolves in order to learn about them. True or false?

....

6 For how many years have people worked and lived with wild animals— 3,000 years or 30,000 years?

....

7 In which U.S. state did Shaun Ellis work with wolves?

....

8 Shark numbers are rising. True or false?

....

9 How do falconers protect their hands?

....

10 What do scientists wear when diving with sharks?

Thrill SEEKERS

Unearth HISTORY

Machu Picchu stands 7,970 ft (2,430 m) above sea level between two mountains. The city had about 200 buildings arranged on wide terraces around a vast central square.

A, B, or C

1 In which country would you find the terra-cotta army?
a China **b** India **c** Burma

2 Chartres Cathedral is famous for which glorious feature?
a Marble Crypt **b** Rose Window **c** Whispering Gallery

3 Catalhöyük was one of the world's earliest towns. Where was it?
a Cyprus **b** Turkey **c** Peru

4 What did the term "treasure trove" mean in its original French form?
a Lost treasure **b** Stored treasure **c** Found treasure

5 Which of these is not the script of an ancient language?
a Elamite **b** Indus **c** Horology

6 Which Roman scholar observed the volcanic eruption that destroyed Pompeii?
a Pliny the Elder **b** Tacitus **c** Marcus Aurelius

7 Where are the Nabataean ruins of Petra?
a Syria **b** Israel **c** Jordan

8 Where did the Vikings originate?
a Albania **b** Latvia **c** Scandinavia

9 Which of these empires originated in West Africa?
a Ashanti **b** Mongol **c** Aztec

10 What name is given to a structure that carries water over a distance?
a Aqueduct **b** Aquifer **c** Aquatint

Picture Clue **Q10**

Unearth HISTORY

True or **False?**

1 In the Middle Ages, a popular sport was for two people to hit each other over the heads with bricks. It was called Brick Bashing.

....

2 Aeschylus, an ancient Greek writer, died when a tortoise fell on his head.

....

3 Romans nailed dead cats to a doorframe to ward off bad weather.

....

4 In ancient Egypt children were only allowed to bathe three times a year.

....

5 Long ago, Chinese baby girls had their feet broken and bound to stop them growing.

....

6 Ancient Greeks attempted to predict the future by studying the insides of dead animals.

....

7 Ancient Egyptian women used to put deadly lead on their faces as a form of make-up.

....

Picture Clue **Q7**

8 In ancient China the punishment for attacking a traveler was to have your hands sewn together.

....

9 In ancient Rome the punishment for being unable to repay debts was to have bits of your flesh cut off by everyone you owed money to.

....

10 Egyptian Pharaohs had servants whose only job was to clean their master's bottom.

ANSWERS 1. False: they used wooden clubs and it was called cudgel play. 2.True: it was dropped by a passing bird. 3. False: they used dead owls instead. 4. False: this rule was followed in Sparta, not Egypt. 5.True. 6.True. 7.True. 8. False: the punishment was having your nose cut off. 9.True. 10.True.

Lucky **Dip**

1 Which came first, the Iron Age or the Bronze Age?

....

2 Early humans are called Homo habilis. What name is given to modern humans?

....

3 Which ancient civilization was ruled by King Nebuchadnezzar II, who conquered Jerusalem?

....

4 Which ancient civilization used a script called hieroglyphics?

....

5 When was the construction of a huge stone circle completed at Stonehenge in England, 2500 BC or 250 BC?

....

6 Which ore did early metal-workers use to extract copper— bauxite or malachite?

....

7 What C do historians use to describe a group of people that have a high level of social, cultural, and technological development?

....

8 What P is a sign that is based on a picture and used in early writing forms?

....

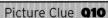

Picture Clue **Q10**

9 Which Pharaoh was buried in the Great Pyramid at Giza?

....

10 Which continent is believed to be the birthplace of the human race?
a Africa **b** Asia **c** Australia

Odd One Out

1 Which of these leaders was not a Roman emperor—Pompey, Augustus, or Severus?

2 An eques was a gladiator who rode a horse. Which weapon was he not allowed to use—a net, a spear, or a sword?

Picture Clue **Q4**

3 Which of these is not a genuine god of ancient Egypt—Seth, Thoth, or Goth?

4 Which feature does not belong in a Gothic cathedral—flying buttress, ribbed vault, or gazebo?

5 Which of these English rulers was never crowned—Matilda, Jane Grey, or Victoria?

6 Who was not a ruler of the Mongol Empire—Kublai Khan, Ghengis Khan, or Khan Noonien Singh?

7 Which of these men did not have children with Cleopatra of Egypt—Julius Caesar, Ptolemy XII, or Mark Anthony?

8 Which of these words is not used to describe an ancient Greek column—Doric, Ionic, or Parabolic?

9 Ting, Ming, Zing—only one of these is the genuine name of a Chinese dynasty. Which one?

10 Which one of these names does not belong to an Aztec Emperor—Moctezuma, Chumbawumba, or Tezozomoc?

ANSWERS 1. Pompey 2. A net 3. Goth 4. Gazebo 5. Matilda 6. Khan Noonien Singh 7. Ptolemy XII 8. Parabolic 9. Ming 10. Chumbawumba

Name the **Number**

1 The Storming of the Bastille was a key event in the history of the French Revolution. In what year did it occur?

....

2 In what year was the American Declaration of Independence signed?

....

3 The twin towers of the World Trade Center were destroyed by a terrorist attack on 9/11, but what was the year?

....

4 Radioactive fallout from an accident at a nuclear power plant in Chernobyl caused widespread fear and contamination. What was the year?

....

5 In what year were the Japanese cities of Nagasaki and Hiroshima targeted with atomic bombs?

....

6 The Great Fire of London began in a baker's shop in Pudding Lane. In what year did this awesome blaze destroy much of the city?

....

7 In which year did HMS *Titanic* sink in just three hours after hitting an iceberg?

....

8 The Hindenburg was an enormous German airship. In what year did it explode, killing 36 people?

....

9 After World War I a flu epidemic killed about 50 million people. In what year was the outbreak?

....

10 In what year did the Cuban Missile Crisis threaten world peace?

Picture Clue **Q8**

Unearth HISTORY

Unearth HISTORY

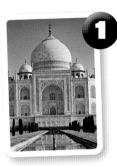

1 I am a marble palace, built between 1630 and 1653. I am believed to be the most beautiful building in the world.

2 I am thousands of miles long. I was originally built as a network of defense against invasion.

3 I was a small seaside town buried with mud and ash by Mount Vesuvius.

4 I am a magnificent ancient temple, dedicated to the Greek goddess Athena.

5 I stand on the bank of the River Thames in London. I am home to the Crown Jewels.

6 I am an ancient royal burial ground in Egypt. Famous discoveries have been made here.

7 I am an ancient site of a great war. in Turkey An epic poem may be based upon what happened here.

8 I am a great temple. For centuries I was central to the Khmer Empire.

9 I was the scene of some of the deadliest battles of World War I. I can be found in France.

13 I am an animal-shaped mound in Ohio, U.S. It is believed that I was built by the Native Americans.

10 Until 1917, I was the official residence of the Russian monarchy. I was built as a symbol of imperial power.

14 I was built in 1961, at the height of the Cold War. I cut a city in half.

11 I am a memorial wall located in Constitution Avenue, Washington D.C. I am covered in over 50,000 names.

15 I am the site of landings by thousands of troops on June 6, 1944.

12 I am a famous ocean liner. I sank on my maiden voyage.

16 I was first reached by Roald Amundsen in 1911. Before the 20th century, I was largely unexplored.

Unearth HISTORY

ANSWERS 1. Taj Mahal 2. Great Wall of China 3. Herculaneum 4. Parthenon 5. Tower of London 6. Valley of the Kings 7. Troy 8. Angkor Wat 9. The Somme battlefields 10. Winter Palace 11. Vietnam Veterans Memorial 12. Titanic 13. The Great Serpent Mound 14. Berlin Wall 15. Normandy beaches 16. South Pole

Starting with P

1 What P is a simple tool that cuts furrows in soil and transformed the development of agriculture?

....

2 What did Gutenberg invent in about 1436?

....

Picture Clue **Q2**

3 Which country gained its independence in 1947, and became an Islamic and Parliamentary Republic in 1956?

....

4 Darius the Great built himself a city—now in modern Iran. What was it called?

....

5 A great thinker of ancient Greece, I am known for many books including *The Republic*. Who am I?

....

6 What giant structures were built on the banks of the Nile as tombs for Egyptian Pharaohs?

....

7 Which red-petalled plant contributed to the Opium Wars?

....

8 Which P describes pots and dishes made of earthenware or baked clay?

....

9 I was the last emperor of China and I came to the throne when I was just two years old. What was my name?

....

10 What name is given to a group of English Protestants who sailed to New England (U.S.) in the 1630s?

Unearth HISTORY

ANSWERS 1. Plough 2. Printing press 3. Pakistan 4. Persepolis 5. Plato 6. Pyramids 7. Poppy 8. Pottery 9. Puyi 10. Puritans

Be a **Genius**

1 This evil emperor adored his horse Incitatus, who was housed in a marble stable and invited to dine with his master's guests.

....

2 Which Roman emperor split the Empire in two to govern it more easily, and then retired to the seaside?

....

3 He loved to watch gladiators so much that this evil ruler liked to join in, although his competitors were given blunt swords.

....

4 The first Christian emperor, he founded the city of Constantinople (now Istanbul).

....

5 He put an end to the Republic, but this emperor created a strong government.

....

6 A great thinker, this emperor ruled from AD 161–180. He wrote a book of meditations.

....

7 A great traveler, this emperor made his empire stronger and even built a mighty wall in Britain.

....

8 Famous for throwing victims off a cliff, this tyrant ruled from AD 14–37.

....

9 He is rumored to have fiddled while Rome burned, and murdered his mother.

....

10 This decadent emperor liked to dress up and behaved so outrageously he was assassinated at the age of just 18.

Picture Clue **Q7**

Unearth HISTORY

ANSWERS 1. Caligula 2. Diocletian 3. Commodus 4. Constantine 1 5. Augustus 6. Marcus Aurelius 7. Hadrian 8. Tiberius 9. Nero 10. Elagabalus

Who am I?

1 In 1847, I took giant statues of lions with human heads from Kalhu (modern-day Iraq) to the British Museum in London, U.K.

....

2 I located and excavated the ancient site of Troy in Hisarlik, Turkey.

....

3 When exploring the Valley of the Kings in southern Egypt in 1922, I discovered Tutankhamun's tomb.

....

4 In 1824, I worked out the three different scripts on the Rosetta Stone.

....

5 In 1978, I uncovered hominid footprints in Laetoli, Tanzania, that are 3.7 million years old.

....

6 I led an expedition in 1911 to Peru, where we discovered the ruins of Machu Picchu.

....

7 In 1812, I rediscovered the lost city of Petra, in Jordan.

....

8 In 1823, I found a skeleton in a cave at Paviland in Wales, U.K. It was from a young male who lived 29,000 years ago.

....

9 I unearthed the palace of Knossos on the Greek island of Crete.

....

10 I helped to decipher Old Persian script, called cuneiform, in the early 1800s.

True or **False?**

1 The study of how early people lived their lives is called anthology.

....

2 The largest hoard of Anglo-Saxon gold and silver ever found was unearthed in Staffordshire in 2009.

....

3 Remains of the ancient city of Troy can be seen in modern Cyprus.

....

4 The Taj Mahal was built as a tomb to commemorate an emperor's love for his wife, Mumtaz Mahal.

....

5 Tutankhamun's golden mask is preserved at the Metropolitan Museum of Art, in New York.

....

6 During the Ming Dynasty (1368–1644), one million soldiers were stationed along the Great Wall of China.

....

7 Cuneiform scripts are made up of wedge-shaped characters.

....

8 The Roman city of Pompeii was destroyed when Mount Etna erupted in AD 79.

....

9 The great temple of Angkor Wat is a popular tourist destination in Vietnam.

Picture Clue **Q8**

....

10 Dry, preserved human bodies are described as being decimated.

ANSWERS 1. False: it is called anthropology. 2. True 3. False: Troy was in Anatolia, in modern Turkey. 4. True 5. False: it is at the Museum of Egyptian Antiquities in Cairo, Egypt. 6. True 7. True 8. False: it was Mount Vesuvius that caused the devastation. 9. False: it is in Cambodia 10. False: they are desiccated.

Picture It

1 What was this building in Rome mainly used for?

2 What is the name for these pillars of stone?

3 These ancient scrolls were found near the shores of which body of water?

4 How many different scripts were found on the Rosetta Stone?

5 Who was president of the United States during World War I?

6 The Step Pyramid was built during which pharaoh's reign?

7 The city of Machu Picchu was built by the Aztecs—true or false?

10 Which country sent an armada to attack England in 1588?

8 Where would you find the Forbidden City?

11 Which queen led an uprising against the Romans in Britain?

9 During the Blitz in World War II, where did thousands of Londoners go for shelter each night?

12 The Crusades were fought in the Middle Ages partly to regain Christian access to which city?

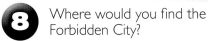

Be a **Genius**

1 Who was the wife of Zeus and Queen of the Olympians?

....

2 How many immortals—called Olympians—lived in a palace on Mount Olympus: 2, 12, or 200?

....

3 Which H was a Greek writer who recorded legends of gods, goddesses, and heroes in the *Iliad*?

....

4 What was the Roman name for Aphrodite, goddess of love, beauty, and fertility?

Picture Clue **Q4**

....

5 Which god gave Midas the power to turn all he touched to gold?

....

6 Hermes was charged with guiding dead souls to the Underworld. What L is a musical instrument he is said to have invented?

....

7 Hephaestus was the Greek god of fire, and called Vulcan by the Romans. What explosive landform did he lend his name to?

....

8 Apollo helped Paris to slay the hero Achilles. What part of Achilles' body was wounded?

....

9 When shown in art, this goddess is often seen carrying a sheath of wheat. Who was she?

....

10 The Olympians took power when they overthrew a race of deities who were descended from Gaia (Earth) and Uranus (Heaven). What were they called?

ANSWERS 1.Hera 2. 12 3. Homer 4.Venus 5. Dionysus 6. Lyre 7.Volcano 8. Heel 9. Demeter 10.Titans

What am I?

1 This Asian city has had many names, including Peking. What is it now called?

....

2 Which Italian city is named in the legend of Romulus and Remus?

....

3 Which beautiful city is built on stilts, and has the Lion of St. Mark for its emblem?

Picture Clue **Q1**

....

4 Maoris lived in this region for 1,000 years before colonists built New Zealand's capital city in 1865. What is the city now called?

....

5 One of the oldest, holiest places in the world, this city is the home to Israel's parliament. What is it called?

....

6 Only Muslims are allowed to visit this holy city of Islam in Saudi Arabia, south of Medina. What is its name?

....

7 This city was home to Pharos, an imposing lighthouse and one of the wonders of the Ancient World. What is it called?

....

8 Which African city was founded in 1652 by the Dutch East India Company, as a supply base for its ships sailing to the East Indies?

....

9 Which ancient city was on the banks of the Niger River, now in modern Mali, and was the capital of Mansa Musa's empire?

....

10 In which city did the Reformation begin, when Martin Luther nailed a list of 95 statements to a church door?

Unearth HISTORY

Lucky **Dip**

1 Which European country developed a passion for growing tulips in the 17th century?

....

2 What A is the revolution that began a transformation in the way that farmers grow food for the world?

....

3 Babur, Akbar, and Jahan were all Mughal emperors of which Asian country?

....

4 What was the name of Captain James Cook's ship that explored the South Pacific—Endeavour or Valour?

....

5 In what year did George Washington become the first president of the U.S.?
a 1789 **b** 1879 **c** 1798

....

6 Where were Shoguns powerful military leaders?

....

7 What name was given to the European war that began in 1756 and lasted for seven years?

....

8 Which religious group began the British anti-slavery movement—the Quakers or the Mormons?

....

9 According to The Bible, how many tribes of Israel were established by Abraham's great-grandsons?

....

10 In what year did French traders and fishermen establish a settlement in Quebec?
a 1608 **b** 1806 **c** 1688

9. 12. 10. 1608

ANSWERS 1. The Netherlands 2. Agrarian or agricultural 3. India 4. Endeavour 5. a 1789 6. Japan 7. The Seven Years' War 8. The Quakers

Who am I?

1 I was a young Egyptian pharaoh and was buried in the Valley of the Kings. My tomb was discovered by Howard Carter.

....

2 My warship, the Mary Rose, sank off the English coast in 1545. I was married to my sixth wife at the time.

....

3 I am called The Iceman because my body was preserved in an Alpine glacier. I was born around 3300 BC.

....

4 I was a Greek God and a temple was built in my honor in Olympia. It is an Ancient Wonder of the World.

....

5 A tomb full of terra-cotta warriors was built to protect me in the afterlife.

....

6 I ruled a Persian Empire, and 50 million people, from 522 to 486 BC. It was the largest empire ever known.

....

7 I was a spiritual leader who lived around 500 BC and my name means "enlightened one." The religion I began has no god.

....

Picture Clue **Q7**

8 The Taj Mahal was built as a tomb for my deceased wife.

....

9 A Muslim leader, I was born in Iraq and defeated the Crusaders at the Battle of Hattin in 1187.

....

10 I was an English soldier and poet who died during World War I. *Anthem for Doomed Youth* is one of my most famous poems.

Unearth HISTORY

ANSWERS 1. Tutankhamun 2. King Henry VIII 3. Ötzi 4. Zeus 5. Emperor Qin Shi Huangdi 6. Darius the Great 7. Buddha (Siddhartha Gautama) 8. Mughal emperor of India, Shah Jahan 9. Saladin 10. Wilfred Owen

MIGHTY
Monuments

Throughout history, people have raised massive buildings, monuments, and statues. The builder's aim has been to create a sense of respect, terror, wonder, or delight. For archeologists, they help to show how past societies lived.

EVERLASTING LOVE

Its white marble walls are inlaid with gems, its tall towers, or minarets, are graceful and slender, and its domes are reflected in still pools of water. This is the Taj Mahal at Agra, India, and it is believed by many to be the most beautiful building in the world. Constructed between 1630 and 1653, it was built as a tomb to commemorate the love Mughal emperor of India, Shah Jahan, felt for his deceased wife, Mumtaz Mahal. In 1666, Shah Jahan also died and was buried next to his wife.

Taj Mahal
Over 1,000 elephants were used to haul marble to the site.

TEMPLE OF THE SERPENT

Chichén Itzá in Mexico was a great city of the Maya and Toltec peoples, occupied between the 8th and 13th centuries AD. In its later years, a great stepped pyramid was built there as a temple to the Feathered Serpent god. A snake, carved in stone, adorns the stairways, and twice each year the Sun casts strange snakelike shadows on the northern steps. The monument later became known in Spanish as el Castillo, meaning "the Castle."

ISLAND GUARDIANS

The first European seafarers to reach the coasts of the remote Pacific island of Rapa Nui ("Easter Island") were mystified by huge stone statues, called Moai. They were carved by the Polynesians who lived between 1200 and 1680. The tallest statue is 33 ft (10 m) high and the heaviest weighs 86 tons.

Chichén Itzá
The pyramid and its platform have one step for each day of the year.

EASTER ISLAND MOAI
887 Moai have survived on Easter Island. They represent ancestors who became gods.

Total **Recall**

1 Where would you find the Moai?

2 For which god is the stepped pyramid in Chichén Itzá built?

3 How many Moai still survive?

4 In what century was the Taj Mahal built?

5 Which people carved the Maoi?

6 The tallest Moai is 100 ft (30 m) tall. True or false?

7 What stone is the Taj Mahal built from?

8 How many elephants were needed to haul the stone to build the Taj Mahal?

9 All of the Moai are older than the Taj Mahal. True or false?

10 How many steps does the Chichén Itzá pyramid have?

Unearth HISTORY

ANSWERS 1. Easter Island (Rapa Nui) 2. Feathered Serpent 3. 887 4. 17th Century 5. Polynesians 6. False: the tallest iss 33 ft (10 m) 7. White marble 8. Over 1,000 9. False: the Taj Mahal was built between 1630 and 1653; the Moai were created between 1200 and 1680

Scorecard

Either photocopy the scorecard or print it from Kids' Corner at www.mileskelly.net. You will need one scorecard per section for each person. Write the quiz numbers in the left-hand column and add a tick for each question you answer correctly. Add up your score for each quiz, then work out your total for the whole section. Are you a quiz master or a quiz dud?

Section																	
Quiz Number	**QUESTIONS**																**Quiz Score**
	1	2	3	4	5	6	7	8	9	10	11	12	13	14	15	16	
Total																	